Trumpet in Zion

Trumpet in Zion

Black Church Worship Resources

Year A

LINDA H. HOLLIES

THE PILGRIM PRESS CLEVELAND, OHIO

Dedication

This work is dedicated to my foremothers:

DORETHA ROBINSON ADAMS

LUCINDA ROBINSON WESTON

EUNICE ROBINSON WADE

LULA SMITH

LOUISE HOLLOWAY

DELLA BURT

HORTENSE HOUSE

REV. DR. JANET HOPKINS

The Pilgrim Press, 700 Prospect Avenue, Cleveland, Ohio 44115-1100
pilgrimpress@ucc.org
216-736-3764

Hollies, Linda H.
    Trumpet in Zion : worship resources / Linda H. Hollies.
        p.   cm.
    Includes bibliographical references.
    Contents: [1] Year A.
    ISBN 0-8298-1410-8 (alk. paper)
    1. African American public worship.   2. Worship programs.   I. Title.

BR563.N4 H653   2001
264'.0089'96073—dc21

2001024585

CONTENTS

PROLOGUE

Theological reflection on Scripture is the work of the people. African American Christians have a deeply rooted tradition of learning, interpreting, reframing, and retelling the biblical story in light of their experiences. We are the people of God who grapple with the meaning of Scripture for our daily lives. We recognize that we are created in the image of God, with intelligence, creative powers, and abilities. We have also been mandated by God to give birth to new images, new beings, and new things. For we are a part of God's continuing creation story.

Trumpet In Zion is a new creation that seeks to address God in the voice, verbiage, and expression of African Americans at worship. Being a product of the Church of God, it has been my joy to wrestle with the lectionary passages and discover the shaded nuances, overt distinctions, and direct linkages to myself, my people, and our journey with God. As a pastor-teacher and faithful student of the living Word, I have delighted in looking at the old, old story through my Africentric, womanist eyes. My picture of and reflection on both God and the Scripture has changed, grown, enlarged, and encompassed more images over the years, due to my education and experiences in the world.

This work is a new resource with a call to worship, call to confession, prayer of confession, words of assurance, responsive reading based on the Psalter, offertory invitation and praise, benediction, and blessing for each Sunday. (Scriptures are taken from the *Revised Common Lectionary, Year A.*) There are points where information is offered for the decoration of the altar around certain themes.

Trumpet In Zion is a "read-to-use" handbook for pastors and worship teams. It is an educational tool, offered to Christian educators for use in church school, confirmation, and small group study. It may be adapted for use by hospital and campus ministers in their settings. And *Trumpet In Zion* is a devotional guide for those who use the lectionary in a systematic fashion. Although the work is set for use with the lectionary, Year A, the materials may be used freely by those who do not follow the lectionary. All parts of the work are compatible for inspiring and promoting personal thoughts to flow from users.

My joy and delight has been the rewriting of the Psalter for use in the African American community. During an Annual Conference Spiritual Formation retreat, we focused on the Psalms, with Dr. Sister Nancy Shrank, author of *Psalms Anew.* Her teaching on the laments of David's community resounded in my spirit. As an assignment was given to rewrite a Psalm for my life, this work was born. *Trumpet In Zion* is my response to God's call to "Cry loud, spare not, lift up your voice, like a trumpet in Zion. Show my people their transgressions, and the house of Jacob their sin." (Isaiah 58:1) These are written as responsive readings to be both the celebrations and laments of worshiping communities.

I am well aware that the limits of this work are due to the boundaries of my world view, education, and life experiences. However, I offer this volume in memory of the ancestors who spoke to God in their own unique, broken, and colorful language; I offer it in celebration of the churches that I have pastored. These faithful souls have allowed me to "practice" liturgies with them each Sunday and on special occasions. I offer it in hope, for the generations that are to follow. They need a record of our praying for them. They need a chronicle of our journey with God.

Rev. Dr. Linda H. Hollies
Lansing, Michigan

P R E F A C E ❀

My writing ability is a gift from God! I recognize that there is no biblical gift specifically named as "the gift of writing." Yet, I am persuaded that my call to paint a rainbow of motions that sketches the old, old story in new and vivid compositions, depicting the picturesque and distinctive world view of people of color, falls under the realm of both pastor-teacher and encourager of the whole people of God. I am awed by and thankful to God for the special endowment of grace that allows me this opportunity.

This particular ministry began with an invitation from the former executive director of National Black Methodists for Church Renewal, Rev. Joseph Roberson. Joe called in November of 1993 and gave me the privilege of drafting the worship service for National Black Methodists for Church Renewal Sunday, 1994. He allowed me full creative flow and I designed the Yam Ceremony, which was utilized by many African American congregations with joy and celebration. That same year, Dr. Walter Willis, board member and director of the Black Pastors Institute, called to request that I design the worship services for this event. From these two occasions, where my peers permitted me to utilize my gifts for speaking the truth in our authentic voice, my colleagues have demanded additional resources. I am eternally grateful to my brothers and sisters who acknowledge my gifts and permit me to be a voice for them. Their encouragement and demand for "more" tap my creative juices and call forth continued movement and growth in me.

Friend and brother Rev. Dr. Myron McCoy was a district superintendent in the Northern Illinois Annual Conference. While active on the District, he enrolled in a Doctor of Ministry program, specifically for district superintendents, at United Seminary in Dayton, Ohio. Because of his personal counsel regarding my growth in professional ministry, I enrolled in their Doctor of Ministry program structured for African American clergy. I was privileged to sit at the feet of two giants in the field of theology, Dr. Jacqueline Grant, Womanist Theology Mentor, and Dr. Dwight

Hopkins, Black Theology Mentor. To interact with, learn from, and be mentored by this awesome team has been thrilling, challenging, and blessed! Their counsel and direction in this work has been invaluable.

I began this journey while serving as one of three pastors at the Arlington Heights First United Methodist Church. I was the first African American pastor to be appointed there and my continued involvement in the life of the black Church was essential. My colleagues there, Rev. Bill Cull and Rev. Dori Baker, were enthusiastic and optimistic about my work. I am indebted to them for their assistance with schedules, insights, and teamwork. They made life easier for me and I love and honor their input into my life and ministry.

The Staff-Parish Committee at First, then chaired by Mr. Rod Jones, enabled the financing of my first year in the program and to them I owe many thanks. In the middle of my work, the Cabinet moved me to the inner city of Chicago. The Southlawn Community United Methodist Church graciously provided continuing education funds and time away to remain in the program. Their active support sanctioned my ministry of writing. The worshiping community at Southlawn provided fertile soil for expanding concepts and ideas to reflect upon the movement of God in our midst.

Writing can consume your time and your energies. I am grateful for the gift of having had both an African American male district superintendent, Bishop Jonathan Keaton, and a white female district superintendent, Rev. Kay Dillard. Both of them have understood and promoted my ministry of writing with the congregations to which I have been appointed. I acknowledge, with thanksgiving, their intervention, assistance, and continuing pastoral care and friendship.

Writing can be a solitary event. Yet, there are individuals in my life whom I cannot do without. The list is headed by my husband, Charles H. Hollies, who takes better care of me than I often deserve. My grandson, Giraurd Chase Hollies, is the joy of my life and my inspiration for the days to come. My children are my motivation for leaving what I have learned documented on paper. Gregory Raymond, Grelon Renard, Grian Eunyke and her children, Gernal Chasad and Symphony, will allow me to live in the coming generations. My siblings push, promote, and support me; they are the essence of "family" at its best: sisters Jacqui Brodie-Davis and Bob; Riene Morris; Regina Pleasant and Arthur; and my brothers Donnie Adams and Jeannette; Eddie Adams and Onnette; David Adams and Kim; and Robert Adams and Lisa.

Robbin Pippin, my editor for "Inner Healing for Broken Vessels" at *Upper Room,* has become a soul-mate. It's her support and recommendation that brought this work to life. She joins a group of sister-friends who nourish my soul: Barbara Vinson; Rev. Vera Jo Edington; Alberta Petrosko; Rev. Daisy Thomas-Quinney; Rev. Dr. Eleanor Miller; Rev. Danita Anderson; Rev. Louisa Martin; Rev. Harlene Harden; Rev. Marie Carlson; Rev. Genevieve Brown; Rev. Michelle Cobb; Rev. Dr. Valerie Davis; Rev. Lillian Gibbs; Rev. Dr. Linda Boston; and Rev. Geraldine Black. Each of these women counsels, prays with and for, challenges, and loves me so that writing flows, preaching continues, and my spirit is renewed. I count each one of these women as blessings, gifts, and treasures in my life. Then, there are my brother-friends, whose love uplifts me and makes me more secure in my position in the family of God. Rev. Anthony Earl, Rev. Dr. Michael Carson, Rev. Dr. Donald Guest, Rev. Dr. Zawdie Abiade, and our adopted son, Rev. Dr. Dennis Robinson, accept me fully as they uphold my life and ministry in their gentle hands. Without them, my life would be so incomplete. But, because of them, I am more wholly alive in the body of Christ.

Writing broadens my community. For now you have become a part of my world! I pray that this work will stimulate you to begin painting your own canvas with wide, happy and life-changing strokes. One of my seminary professors and friend, Dr. Emma Justes, taught me that the Bible not only speaks to us, but speaks about us, individually! Every one of us can encounter our God and ourselves anew, as we read and reflect upon the living Word. May the word pictures of your meditative rendezvous with the Scriptures change your world! Shalom, my friends!

1 · **Overview**

John Brown Russwurm was the publisher of the first black-owned newspaper in the United States. In the very first editorial of *Freedom's Journal,* March 16,1827, he wrote: "We wish to plead our own cause. Too many others have spoken for us. Too long has the public been deceived by misrepresentations in things which concern us dearly. . . ."[1] This same reason has prompted me to struggle with the lectionary and find the means to paint word pictures that would clearly represent the world of Christians of color.

Trumpet In Zion is a pleading of our own cause with God. It is one attempt to "have a little talk with Jesus, to tell him all about our troubles!"[2] And we will tell him in our own unique, soulful, and colorful way. We are a people who have been faithful to the realm of God. We have labored and served and remained without undue fuss or bother. When mistreated, we forgive. When misunderstood, we explain. When denied, we wait. When overlooked, we stay. When passed over, we return. When needed, we serve. And, in our pain, we tell it to Jesus! We tell him, for "he will hear our faintest cry and answer by and by!"[3] We tell him, for it is difficult to be talked about, pushed aside, neglected, rejected, abused, used, and overlooked in every facet of life. We have always had "our say," to Jesus Christ! It needs to be written and preserved for the generations to follow.

Trumpet In Zion will plead our cause, not as second-class Christians, but as people with both a mission and a message. We will plead our cause as those with a deep and abiding faith in the God of the ancestors. We will plead our cause as a nation called, chosen, preserved, and delivered by God for "such a time as this!" We will plead our cause, in our own voice, articulating our own reality and having a dialogue with our own God. The validity of our experiences with God demands that we have our own say!

Black author and poet Margaret Walker has said, "there is a rumbling in the land."[4] The wave of Africentric consciousness is sweeping the land. Africentric thought moves the focus of our standards and actions from European ideals to African thoughts and models. Africentric studies in schools, universities, and seminaries have opened the eyes of many to our link to African roots, without shame or apology. We have grown from simply being "black," with no land to claim or history, except that of slavery and the cotton fields.

Today, African Americans look back to a heritage rich in tradition, culture, dress, and patterns of worship. Unifying African-centered thought and behavior has created a rumbling within our souls. The cruel and oppressive conditions we have endured and continue to face; the journey from our home to these shores; and the denial of our pain-filled reality now demand a loud and public voice. We have lived, worked, loved, sacrificed, created, worshiped, struggled, and endured without telling the truth of our own story! For too long we have attempted to allow others to be "the" voice in the liturgical work of the Church.

But the Africentric rumbling demands that we unveil our own truth. A *Trumpet In Zion* is another expression of having our say as we have a little talk with Jesus!

2 · The Advent Season

Advent means Mary is pregnant! This is our time to prepare for the Christmas Day birth. The announcement leads us into a season of cleaning up the mangers of our hearts. Advent is our time to wait as we prepare for the arrival of Christ.

The angel comes to the priest who cannot receive the great promise. He is silenced during the wait. The angel goes to a virgin girl who says "Yes" to the great promise. She is silent as she walks to the home of the priest and his pregnant wife. When the pregnant wife goes to greet the silent virgin, the Holy Spirit descends and singing and dancing begin. Elizabeth is filled with the Holy Spirit. Mary sings Hannah's old song. John the Baptist dances in his mother's womb. And the world waits for the birth!

It's been a long wait since the Hebrew prophets foretold this virgin birth. During these weeks of Advent, as Mary prepares to bring forth her firstborn child, tell the old stories of a faithful God who is a promise keeper. Tell the old stories of how God got silent for more than 400 years and decided to speak to the waiting world through the bellies of two pregnant women. During Advent, tell the stories of how we wait for new hope, new birth, and new life!

Altar Focus

The idea is to build the altar each week, beginning with a scene that speaks to the congregation about waiting, watching, preparing, and hope. Positioning a glass star to twinkle over an empty shelter, representing a barn, could begin Week One. Week Two, animals might be placed in strategic places. Week Three, an empty manger can be brought center stage, along with different types of shepherds. Week Four, the parental figures of Mary and Joseph can be seen.

On Christmas Eve, an array of angels might be appropriate, along with many different types of candles representing the light that is to come. The infant figure does not appear until Christmas Day. I suggest you place a large loaf of brown bread in the manger. Jesus is the bread of life and was born to die. It is not appropriate for us simply to get misty-eyed over the babe in the manger, without realizing the fullness of his Advent.

A way to include the congregation in the building of the altar and the spirit of anticipation will be to ask them to bring animals, shepherds, and angels from home. After the lighting of the Advent candle, these gifts can be brought forward.

Many churches place poinsettias around the altar for the Christmas Eve worship. They should not detract from the focus of the worship setting. Sufficient room always needs to be left for the sacrament to be placed. Beauty ought never compromise our true and authentic worship!

THE FIRST SUNDAY OF ADVENT

Isaiah 2:1–5
Psalm 122
Romans 13:11–14
Matthew 24:36–44

Call to Worship

Leader: The Liberator is on his way!
People: We are awaiting his arrival.
Leader: The Liberator will arrive soon!
People: Blest be the name of our God who comes.
Leader: Lift up your hearts in worship.
All: We celebrate the Deliverer of Zion! Amen.

Hymn of Celebration for Advent

("Mary Had a Little Lamb"[5] Slow beat to the standard melody)
Mary had a little lamb, a little lamb, a little lamb.
Mary had a little lamb and Jesus was his name.
He was born in Bethlehem, in Bethlehem, in Bethlehem.
He was born in Bethlehem, the Son of God by name.
Miracles he came to do, came to do, came to do.
Miracles he came to do, for me and for you.

Candle Lighting

We are a waiting people. Our hearts have grown weary during the year. It seems as if we have been forgotten and left to fight for our freedom all alone. But Advent has come, the wait is almost over. In eager anticipation we light this candle, a symbol of our expectant waiting.

Call to Confession

Leader: Oftentimes the pain of waiting causes us discouragement. In our discouragement we begin to doubt that God really does care. Let us confess our pain before a listening God.
All: Ancient of Days, we confess that Jesus told us to prepare ourselves for doing great things, and too often we have fooled around, majoring in

minor issues. Isaiah called us to hammer our swords into plowshares and be finished with fighting. Yet, we daily fight enemies, both within and without. Forgive us our sin. Help us to see that heaven's ear is open to us and that you are in every place, seeing the evil and the good. Help us to believe that our waiting is not in vain. Fill us, we pray, with a fresh vision of shalom. Amen.

Silent Confession

Words of Assurance

Rise! Shine! Your deliverance has come! The glory of our God is revealed and all of us will see it together. And, this is good news! Amen.

Responsive Reading Psalm 122

Leader: I was glad when they said unto me, "Let us go to the house of the Lord!"

People: We stand in this place of sanctuary, the house that God's name upholds.

Leader: This house is bound firmly together. We are the tribes of the diaspora—scattered to the four winds. But, in this place of refuge, we give thanks to our Redeemer and Deliverer.

People: We pray for the peace of our nation.

Leader: May all prosper who love our God. The shalom of Zion is within these walls, here we are secure. Let's bless the name of God.

People: For the sake of the ancestors and our future generations, I declare, "Shalom is with us!" Amen!

Offertory Invitation

There are needs everywhere and few of us have an overabundance from which to give. But, in the spirit of Mary and Joseph, who risked what they had to secure our salvation, let us share together.

Offertory Praise

Generous God, we thank you for these signs of hope. We have returned to you a small portion of all you've given unto us. We pray that some motherless child, some lonely senior citizen, or some homeless individual might also reap a harvest of blessing from what we have sown in your name. Amen.

Doxology

(Sung to tune of "Old 100th")
Praise God from whom all blessings flow.
We wait in anticipation here below.
Praise God for signs of love and care.
For God's Emmanuel is everywhere! Amen!

Benediction

Leader: Waiting without hope is torture.
People: Waiting without help produces fear.
Leader: But our hope is in the God who does come.
People: And our help is in the God who is here!
Leader: So we wait, expectantly, for the God who will come again.
People: For we know that the Liberator is on the way!
Leader: Leave in that power and with his peace!
All: Amen and amen!

THE SECOND SUNDAY OF ADVENT

Isaiah 11:1–10
Psalm 72:1–19
Romans 15:4–13
Matthew 3:1–12

Call to Worship

Leader: Today, we are watching for signs of God's arrival.
People: Lord, prepare me to be a sanctuary.[6]
Leader: We can see the outward signs of preparation.
People: Lord, prepare me to be a sanctuary.
Leader: We recognize that decorated trees, electric stars, and glitter will soon lose their attraction.
People: Lord, prepare me to be a sanctuary, acceptable for your arrival.
Leader: With clean hearts and watchful eyes, let's worship God in spirit and in truth.
All: Alleluia! Amen!

Candle Lighting

We are a watching people! We have a history of watching for approaching enemies, those who arrive in the night to do their dirt. We have watched for bill collectors and rip-off artists, who have stolen from us, without guns. We have watched as other ethnic groups have moved up and on. We have watched as systems have worked to push us aside and keep us away from the flow of justice and equality. But today, we watch for our Savior's coming. And, we light this candle as a symbol of the Hope of the World. Even so, come, Lord. Come quickly to our aid. Amen.

Call to Confession

God of the watch, it is to you that we turn in confession. You keep watch over Zion and neither slumber nor sleep. Forgive us for closing our eyes to your promises. Forgive us for neglecting to see signs of your coming in our world, your Church, and our own lives. Forgive us for feeling that you have failed to be faithful to us, when in reality, we have been the unfaithful ones! Forgive us our sin. Open our eyes. Let us see your salvation and participate in preparing your way. Amen.

Silent Confession

Words of Assurance

God is a good God! God is a great God! God can do anything but fail. God has already moved mountains out of our way; we know we can trust this wonderful and watchful God! Amen.

Responsive Reading Psalm 72:2–7, 18–19

Leader: All-seeing Majesty, call the world's leaders to justice.
People: Speak your righteous standards to those in charge of political and religious affairs.
Leader: May your sons and daughters, everywhere, be treated with righteousness and allow the oppressed to be delivered speedily. Defend the poor, grant mercy to the needy, and bring down every oppressive force.
People: We praise you for the gift of Christ, who outshines the sun and moon throughout all generations.
Leader: May the reign of Christ vindicate us and cause justice to run like water, and righteousness like ever-flowing streams.
People: Blessed be God, the protector of all who trust. May our awesome God's glory fill the earth! Amen.

Offertory Invitation

God has granted us favor and protection. We have been chosen and called children of the Most High. What will we render as evidence of our appreciation and gratitude?

Offertory Praise

God of abundance, you have everything and sent us Jesus Christ to make us heirs to it all. We return only a token pledge of our grateful stewardship. May it be used to make straight paths for both the young and old. Amen.

Benediction

Leader: Servants, keep watch; the hour is far spent.
People: Our eyes are open; our hearts are prepared.

Leader: Servants, keep watch; the Bridegroom is coming.

People: Our lamps are trimmed and burning.

Leader: Servants, keep watch; the High God who brought you this far continues to watch over the journey.

People: We leave, confident and assured of God's all-seeing eye! Alleluia and amen!

THE THIRD SUNDAY OF ADVENT

Isaiah 35:1–10
Luke 1:47–55
James 5:7–10
Matthew 11:2–11

Call to Worship

Leader: Prepare the way! Make straight paths for God's Son.
People: How do we know this is the One? Perhaps there is another.
Leader: Prepare the way! This is the Word made flesh, our brother and our friend.
People: How do we know this is the One? Are you sure there is no other?
Leader: This is Mary's little boy child, born in a manger and sent to Africa, in exile.
People: Oh, this is the Incognito God, who hides in our colored skins, knows our broken language, and has suffered our undeserved pain!
Leader: Prepare the way! This is the shield of our ancestors, the Lion of the Tribe.
People: We bow in humble submission to worship our God. Amen.

Candle Lighting

We are called to prepare the way for a hidden God. We look for our gods to have power, money, and position. We want our gods to be big and strong, able to defend us and make us feel secure. We don't look among the weak and the defenseless for a god. We don't seek any god among the poor and the oppressed. No one would look for God in a stable and surely they never conceived of God coming out of Africa! But today we light this candle as we prepare for our surprising and amazing God, who continues to appear in the most unexpected places and among the least favorable of persons.

Call to Confession

Oftentimes, it is not God who hides, but us. Let us confess the hidden sin in our lives

Silent Confession

Words of Assurance

The Holy One's eye is in every place, beholding the evil and the good. It is God's good pleasure to give us an eternal realm! Confession puts us in the posture to receive. Amen.

Responsive Reading Luke 1:47–55

Leader: My soul magnifies the Lord, and my spirit rejoices in God, my Savior.

People: The Proclaimer of Justice has looked with favor on the state of lowly servants. Surely, from now on, all generations shall be astonished at our blessedness in God.

Leader: The mighty Lion of our tribe has done great things for us. Holy is the name of our God.

People: The Keeper of our souls shows mercy from generation to generation on those who offer reverence and obedience.

Leader: Our God is a strong god, who will judge the haughty and the irreverent.

People: The record of the Eternal One gives evidence that those who were once powerful, in their own eyes, have been erased from the world's history.

Leader: But the meek, the lowly, and the insignificant, God lifts up to high places.

People: God is food in a starving land and water in dry places. The poor become rich and the rich become empty in the scheme of a just and loving God.

Leader: The Hope of the World has promised our ancestors mercy. We live in that state of promise.

People: The Covenant God remembers our plight. That is mighty good news! Amen.

Offertory Invitation

How do we prepare to receive the world's greatest gift? We prepare by giving. "Give and it shall be given unto you, pressed down, shaken together, and running over . . ." is the promise of what we shall receive.

Offertory Praise

Generous God, you give the sun for light and the water for dry places. It is of your generosity that we offer back to you a share. May these offerings help the desert places to bloom and the high places to be brought low. For we give in the name of your great gift to us, Jesus the Christ. Amen.

Benediction

Leader: Beloved, prepare yourself for the coming of the Lord.

People: We will strengthen weak hands and make firm our feeble knees.

Leader: Say to those of a fearful heart, "Be strong! The hour of the Lord is near."

People: The ransomed of the Lord shall return and come to Zion with singing; everlasting joy shall be upon our heads. We leave with gladness and singing.

Leader: May the Comforter of Zion keep you until we meet again. Amen.

THE FOURTH SUNDAY OF ADVENT

Isaiah 7:10–16
Psalm 80:1–19
Romans 1:1–7
Matthew 1:18–25

Call to Worship

Leader: Listen! A virgin is pregnant.
People: How can this be?
Leader: The Holy Spirit is responsible!
People: But why?
Leader: For God promised us a Savior, a deliverer, a liberator, to save us from our sin.
People: What is his name?
Leader: Some call him Emmanuel, some Prince of Peace, others, the Unexplainable God.
People: When can we meet him?
Leader: In this very room, the Hope of the world is present. So come, let us adore him!
People: He is Christ the Lord!

Candle Lighting

Sometimes it is difficult to hope; when the economy is in a downtrend and we are yet the last hired and first fired. Sometimes it is difficult to hope; when our communities are war zones and it's our own children who frighten us the most. Sometimes it is difficult to hope; when the crisis of drugs, gangs, and violence seems to be on the upswing, in spite of our concerns and our prayers. But, since we are people of faith, we light this candle of hope. It is a symbol that our fearful hearts remain fixed on Christ, the Hope of the world.

Call to Confession

Leader: When our hope is dim, our worship is shallow and insufficient. Let us confess our sin before a loving and trustworthy God.

All: Ever-Pregnant and Birthing God, we confess our miscarriage of the hope that you provide. Often we deliberately abort your dreams for us by neglecting the new life within. Sometimes we allow the gift to wither and die because of our fear of the pains of giving birth. Whatever the reason, it is sin, and we repent. Forgive us for not trusting you to bring to life the hopeful starts you plant within us. Restore us to faithful and authentic worship and praise. Amen.

Words of Assurance

All day long God lies on a maternity bed giving birth to hopes, dreams and new visions! New life is available to us now. This is good news! Amen.[7]

Responsive Reading Psalm 80:1–7, 17–19

Leader: Shepherd of Zion, hear our cry. You are the beacon to those of the diaspora. Shine on us and come quickly to our aid.
People: Let the light from your lighthouse shine on us![8]
Leader: God we plead for restoration, that your glory may be seen and we might be saved.
People: Let the light from your lighthouse shine on us!
Leader: Lord of Hosts, how long will you allow our prayers to go unanswered?
People: Let the light from your lighthouse shine on us!
Leader: You have given us over to tears, too many to measure!
People: Let the light from your lighthouse shine on us!
Leader: We are the scorn of the earth, harassed, ridiculed, and mocked. Our status is often made a laughingstock.
People: Let the light from your lighthouse shine on us!
Leader: God of Zion, send your spirit of refreshing! Let your face shine upon us, whom you have made in your image and likeness and called "very good!"!
People: Let the light from your lighthouse shine on us!
Leader: Validate our suffering. Elevate our hopes. Uplift our situation. Give us new life! For we call upon your redeeming name.
People: Hope of the World, shine in us. Let the light from your lighthouse shine on us! Amen.

Offertory Invitation

Mary, a young, unwed virgin girl, risked all she had to contribute to the salvation drama.

Today, God is yet calling for risk takers! The story of salvation is yet unfolding, let's do our part in sharing.

Offertory Praise

The gift of Jesus Christ is yet mystery and mysterious in our midst. Why would he come from heaven to share in our life and pain? This type of love overwhelms us and leaves us scratching our heads. But, God, we are thankful and offer these meager gifts in return. Use them, we pray, to help prepare the way of the Lord. Amen.

Benediction

Leader: Hearing and seeing, leaping and running, go into the world.
People: We go with joy to prepare for the birth of the Christ.
Leader: Spread the good news, for many need to know that salvation is in the Coming One.
People: We will share what we have received with the communities in which we live and work.
Leader: Tell it, shout it, and proclaim him everywhere.
People: Jesus Christ is Lord, to the glory of God! Alleluia and amen!

3 · The Christmas Season

The Hope of the world is Jesus! We celebrate his moving into our skin, sharing our humanity, and winning for us the victory over death, the grave, and hell. Christmas is not simply one day. Christmas is a season of sharing the mystery of God's love made manifest in Jesus Christ. Christmas is a season of wonder, where the Babe in Bethlehem captures the attention of the whole world. Christmas is the season of new hope, new joy, and a newfound sense of community. May this be a Mary's Christmas for you and your congregation! Look for the angels. Watch for the stars. Prepare for the shepherds. Be in tune with the angelic songs. Open your heart and allow there to be room in the inn of your heart!

Christmas is the season that leads us into Epiphany, where we are urged to be on the lookout for signs of Christ's presence in our midst.

CHRISTMAS DAY · PROPER 1

Isaiah 9:2–7
Psalm 96
Titus 2:11–14
Luke 2:1–20

Call to Worship

Leader: Arise! Shine! Let's give God glory and praise!
People: We who have walked in gloom have experienced a new light. Jesus Christ the Lord is born!
Leader: Yokes have been broken, the rod of the oppressor is smashed, and slavery is abolished forever!
People: A child has been born, a Son given unto us. Power and authority are invested in him.
Leader: His name is Wonderful Counselor, Mighty God, Everlasting Creator, and Prince of Peace.
People: This God of shalom is our God and Zion will forever worship, in spirit and in truth. Amen.

Lighting the Christ Candle

It's an awesome story, this birth of a babe in Bethlehem. It's been told over and over again. Homeless parents, with no family around, are forced to have their child in a stable, filled with animals and awful smells. The Child of Peace is laid in a manger, signifying that he is food for the hungry and bread in a starving land. This infant was born to die! The stars danced, the angels sang a cantata, and animals bowed low in humble submission, representing us before the lover of our souls. We light this candle today, because we were not there to participate in the birthday party of the Son of the Most High God. But when he comes again, we will be present!

Call to Confession

On this holy day, our hearts need to be the cradle of love, tenderly holding the Savior of the world. Let our confession prepare us for this awesome duty.

Silent Confession

Words of Assurance

For us, Mary had a little Lamb, and Jesus is his name! Thanks be unto God. Amen.

Responsive Reading Psalm 96:1–10

Leader: Let's sing unto the Lord a new song!
People: Our God is an awesome God![9]
Leader: Bless the Lord, tell of this great salvation from day to day.
People: What a mighty God we serve![10]
Leader: Declare the Sovereign's glory among the people.
People: Our God reigns![11]
Leader: Great is the Lord, greatly to be praised!
People: Go, tell it upon the mountain![12]
Leader: Honor and Majesty, Strength and Beauty are strong names of God in this sanctuary.
People: Come by here, good Lord![13]
Leader: Give the Power that Saves, glory. Bring an appropriate offering of thanksgiving.
People: What shall I render?[14]
Leader: Simply worship the Lord, in the beauty of holiness. For our God reigns![15]
People: Ain't dat good news![16] Amen!

Offertory Invitation

The grace of God has appeared, bringing salvation to us all. While we have waited for this blessed hope, today is the manifestation of God's abundant and abounding love for us. While we were yet sinners, God loved us and sent Jesus to be born, just to die for us! God has already given unto us. Let us now respond to this glorious gift.

Offertory Praise

Glory to God in the highest and on earth, peace! Thank you, Amazing God, for giving us eternal life in Jesus Christ. May our offerings spread the compassion, the healing, and the work of justice that his coming announced and his ministry proclaimed. Amen!

Benediction

Leader: Joy to the world, the Lord is come![17]

People: We leave to spread this good news.

Leader: Joy to the world, the Lord is in you!

People: Thanks be to God for this immeasurable gift.

Leader: Joy to the world, the Lord will come again!

People: We will proclaim this message in our lives.

Leader: The grace of God and the sweet communion of the Holy Spirit and the love of the Child who came to die, go with you. Alleluia and amen!

CHRISTMAS · PROPER 2

Isaiah 62:6–12
Psalm 97
Titus 3:47
Luke 2:8–20

Call to Worship:

Leader: Holy people, redeemed of the Lord, the Christ Child has arrived.
People: Glory, honor, power, and majesty is the praise upon our lips.
Worthy is the Lamb of God!
Leader: Let the earth be glad and the coasts sing with joy.
People: It is a Mary's Christmas. She has been delivered. Jesus is among us.
All: This is a celebration of joyful hearts. Thanks be to God.

Lighting the Christ Candle

Our salvation has come. Our reward for the long wait has arrived. God has sought us in our sin, helped us to clear out the mangers of our hearts, and helped us be ready to receive this visit from Jesus. We light this candle in honor of his arrival.

Call to Confession

The Lord loves those who hate evil. God guards and preserves the faithful. Let the confession of our sin rescue us from the coming judgment of God.

Confession

God, your goodness and kindness have appeared to us in Jesus Christ. Your holy child has put on our flesh and moved into our human community. Let the radiant light of your glory sweep upon our hearts. Forgive our sin. Remove all that is unpleasing to you. Make us worthy mangers for your presence. In the name of Christ we pray. Amen.

Words of Assurance

God's mercy endures to all generations. By the renewing power of the Holy Spirit we are washed clean and made ready to host The Savior. This is good news.

Responsive Reading Psalm 97

Leader: There is a ruler in the hood!
People: We have a need to shout and celebrate.
Leader: The posse of the ruler includes the twins of right living and justice. They ride ahead to clear the way.
People: There is a ruler in the hood!
Leader: The whole earth trembles, even the mountains melt like wax.
People There is a ruler in the hood!
Leader: Heaven sent the announcement. Things will be put in order.
People: This is a glorious day of victory. There is a ruler in the hood and King Jesus is his name. We his people shout out our praise.

Offertory Invitation

Joseph and Mary gave all they had. It is now required of us that we share in the task of joyous giving. Our giving says we want there to always be room in the inn for the Christ.

Offertory Praise

The power of the Holy Spirit has been poured out so richly upon us in Jesus Christ, our Savior. We give these gifts in the thanksgiving that others may become heirs to the hope of eternal life.

Benediction

Leader: The angelic choir has hushed. The shepherds have gone back to work. The manger has been returned to the stable animals. Only our hearts now hold the One who was born to die. Go into the world, telling all that the Savior has indeed been born in you.
People: The shalom of Christ is ours to spread.
All: Thanks be to God!

CHRISTMAS · PROPER 3

Isaiah 52:7–10
Psalm 98
Hebrews 1:1–12
John 1:1–14

Call to Worship:

Leader: Step lively! Step lively! God enjoys lovely feet.
People: What's up with the feet and the stepping? It's Sunday morning!
Leader: So right you are my sisters and brothers. How beautiful are the feet of those who will tell the news that our God reigns.
All: With praise upon our lips and rejoicing in our feet, we'll step lively to inform the world that Christ is born in us!

Candle Lighting

The Holy Arm of the Lord is revealed through the birth of Jesus Christ. We light this candle to announce the good news with joy!

Call to Confession

Jesus is the reflection of God's glory and the exact imprint of God's very being. With our confession of sin that holy image is seen in us. Let us pray.

Confession

We fess up! For surely we have messed up. We've spent too much on the material stuff of this holy season. Today we ask forgiveness of the sin that controls us. Cleanse us and sustain by your Living Word, the Christ. In the name of Jesus Christ we pray.

Words of Assurance

Long ago God spoke to our ancestors in multiple and various ways. On this Christmas Day God speaks to us by the coming of the Beloved Son. This is good news.

Responsive Reading Psalm 98

Leader: Turn up the decibel. Pump up the praise. It's new song time in the house!

People: We have new songs to offer unto the Lord. For new blessings have been received. New mercy has been extended.

Leader: We have the victory! Despite situations and circumstances that appears to the contrary, this day is a shout out for victory!

People: The whole earth is glad and filled with melodies of praise.

Leader: The Maestro of Music deserves to be lifted up.

People: We will make a joyful noise unto the Lord. Turn up the decibels, for we are turning up the praise!

Offertory Invitation

The oil of gladness is our gift today. Let our giving reflect our grateful hearts.

Offertory praise

God is the same. God's years will never end. For the constant and faithful gifts we have received, we offer back a portion in thanks. To God be the glory. Amen.

Benediction

Leader: The Word is flesh.

People: The Word came to us.

Leader: The Word is flesh.

People: The Word lives among us.

Leader: The Word is flesh.

People: The Word lives in us.

Leader: Go! Be living testimonies that Jesus is alive forevermore!

All: We leave in the power of the Living Word. Amen.

THE FIRST SUNDAY AFTER CHRISTMAS

Isaiah 63:7–9
Psalm 148
Hebrews 2:10–18
Matthew 2:13–23

Call to Worship

Leader: Let us recall the gracious deeds of the Lord.
People: Our God has done great things for us and we are glad.
Leader: God has been merciful and steadfast in love.
People: For all that we have undergone this year, in spite of our tribulations and persecutions, God has been faithful.
Leader: God has not sent angels or messengers to come and see about us and our plight. But the God of all times and places has come instead!
People: We worship because God is in our midst!

Lighting the Christ Candle

How often others have sent messages of condolence about our situations; some have sent money, thinking it would absolve their guilt. There have been many who have come to live among us, trying all the while to make us look and behave like them. But God saw us as we were and loved us for whose we are. We light this candle in gratitude of the Inexhaustible One who always comes with acceptance.

Call to Confession

Leader: Brothers and sisters, because we have historically been a suffering people, we tend to identify with the oppressor and hate those who look like us. Let us confess our sin before the Searcher of our hearts.
All: Suffering One, we confess the many times and diverse ways you have suffered to bring us to your glory. We confess our hesitation to identify with you, the pioneer of our salvation through sufferings. Forgive us our sin. Let your grace and forgiveness touch us, cleanse us, and help us to see you more clearly and to love you, ourselves, and each other, more dearly. Through the exalted Christ, we pray. Amen.

Silent Confession

Words of Assurance

Jesus has come, not to help pious, angelic beings, but to redeem, set free, and uplift the descendents of Abraham, Sarah, and Hagar. Jesus became like us to become for us the sacrificial atonement for our sins. Because he was tested by what he suffered, he is able to help us in our testings. This is good news!

Responsive Reading Psalm 148

Leader: Praise the Lord! Praise the abundant God.
People: For a bountiful harvest and celebration of first fruits, we praise God.
Leader: For the power of community and its call to unity, let's praise God.
People: Our God created the first garden, gave it to the ancestors, and charged them to be fruitful and to multiply. We are their heritage.
Leader: For community and the gift of each other, God is worthy of praise.
People: Every mountain, hill, cedar, oak; wild animal, cattle, creeping and flying thing is a gift to be cherished and preserved.
Leader: Young men and women, elders and seasoned ones, self-determination, perseverance, and purpose are in our hands.
People: Bring the mat, light the menorah, and lift up the cup of salvation. As we honor the past and plan for the future, remember the High God who has raised a cornucopia of treasures for us in our present times.
Leader: People of the diaspora, God's glory is with us!
People: Praise the Lord!

Offertory Invitation

Our farmland is disappearing; the days of planting, tilling, and cultivating belong primarily to yesterday. Yet God continues to provide us with a different type of harvest, from which we are blessed to share.

Offertory Praise

Multiplying God, of farm and factory, lush tropics and urban blight, we offer you the labor of our hands and the fruit of our harvest, in humble thanks for your provisions and care. Amen.

Benediction

Leader: May the Lord of the harvest bless you!
People: May the Spirit of community bind us in unity.
Leader: May the Spirit of love send you to neighbors, co-workers, and unchurched family members.
People: We will go, because God came to us!
Leader: Go in the peace and power of God.
People: We leave to be Christ, alive, in the world! Alleluia and amen!

WATCH NIGHT WORSHIP · DECEMBER 31

Deuteronomy 28:1–14
Psalm 90
John 1:1–14
Hebrews 13:1–17

This is a service of African American congregations that began as people anticipated "watching out" the last year of slavery. The service of watching and waiting continues.

Watch night worship is a time for reflection, testimonies, and songs of God's grace. It is the period when we voice our determination for the gift of a year to come. Usually an intergenerational service, both youth and seasoned saints can play an important part. History meets the future. Tradition faces hopes. The God of the years is constant. Jesus is the same yesterday, today, and forever.

Altar Focus

A big clock with the hands stuck at five minutes to midnight sits on an altar covered with red, black and green kente cloth. Implements of grinders, hoes, spades, and even an old cotton sack become the visual aids. A quilt draping the altar would be another useful article. Stalks of wheat, bolls of cotton, and even tobacco leaves can be placed in vases as "floral" arrangements.

Time is optional, of course. However, the ideal gathering is around a potluck dinner with games for all ages following. Worship should be begin around 10:30 P.M. Serving breakfast following worship allows the guns of salute to stop and the revelers to find their way inside!

Call to Worship

Leader: Why do we gather on this night?
People: We gather to remember our enslaved past.
Leader: Why do we gather on this night?
People: We gather to celebrate God's keeping powers.
Leader: Why do we gather on this night?

People: We gather to recall God's mercies in the midst of oppression.
Leader: Why do we gather this night?
People: We gather to celebrate our God who journeys with us, year by year.
All: Thanks be unto the ever faithful and true God.

Song of Praise

Call to Confession

Leader: The year is almost over. Many of the things we made covenant to do in January have fallen by the wayside. Let us seek forgiveness of our sin.

Silent Confession

Words of Assurance

Our sins are removed as far as the east is from the west. This is the promise of God. For our God yearns for authentic relationship with us. This is mighty good news.

Call to Remember

Remember God's goodness during the year. Many are the afflictions of the righteous, but the Lord delivers us from them all. Those with willingness are provided these moments to testify to the ways God has sent victory our way.

Call to Prayer for the New Year

The year is almost over. Our elders taught us how to bow on our knees before the Almighty. Kneeling conveys our humble attitude before God. Kneeling is a symbol of our grateful hearts before the throne of Grace. Let us prepare now to kneel in prayer as we watch for the New Year. Let us praise God together on our knees.

A Covenant of Declarations

Leader: Happy New Year! Thank God for another opportunity to offer praise and thanksgiving to our Maker, Redeemer, and Sustainer. Resolutions often last until after breakfast! But our foreparents made their declarations of intentions for better Christian service as they were empowered by the Holy Spirit. As you are led, please rise and state your intentions to walk with Jesus in this New Year.

Offertory Invitation

Through the year God has been faithful. Our generous response through our sharing is how we say, "Thanks."

Offertory Praise

Beneficent and Gracious Savior, we cannot pay for one second of the year you have brought us through. Yet, we offer these tokens in humble appreciation that as others watch and wait in the coming years, these doors will be open to receive their grateful hearts. In the name of Love we pray.

Benediction

Leader: The old has passed and the New Year has arrived.
People: We have a new beginning.
Leader: The Lord of fresh starts has given us a brand new slate.
People: We leave to write new history with our Amazing God.
Leader: Go in the peace and power of the God who holds yesterday, today, and every tomorrow. Remember, you are blessed signs of God's renewing promises as you go your way rejoicing!
People: Amen.

HOLY NAME OF JESUS DAY · JANUARY 1

Numbers 6:22–27
Psalm 8
Galatians 4:47 or Philippians 2:5–11
Luke 2:15–21

Call to Worship

Leader: The Name Above All Names summons us today.
People: We have heard the calling of our names.
Leader: The Name Beyond Words commands an accounting.
People: We have heard the calling of our names.
Leader: The Name Above All Names has given us a new name.
People: We bless the wonderful name of Jesus!

Call to Confession

Too often we fail to live up to the name Christian. Confession restores the worth and value of our name. Let us offer our prayers of confession.

Confession

God, you have called us by name. Like children, at times we act as if we do not hear our names being called. Forgive us our sin. Restore us to full relationship with you. We long to walk worthy of your matchless name. It is in the name of Jesus that we pray.

Words of Assurance

We have been made in the image of God. We have been crowned with glory and honor. With our confession of sin we receive restoration of the right to bear the name. Glory to the majestic name of our Sovereign God.

Offertory Invitation

We are children of God, adopted into the royal family. We are heirs to salvation. It is our right to share in order that others may know about this wonderful relationship.

Offertory Praise

Lavishly Generous One, you have given us everything, including the right to wear the name of the Only Begotten Son. Accept these, our gifts that others might come to wear and to bless his exalted name. In the name of Christ we pray. Amen.

Responsive Reading Psalm 8

Leader: God's name is a household word.
People: In all places across town the name of God is uplifted.
Leader: Babies and toddlers, primary youth, and rapping teens all call on the name of God.
People: Not all talk of God is holy!
Leader: Some God language is very profane.
People: Parents call upon the name of God.
Leader: Grandparents pray the name of God.
People: Sophisticated folks tip around this blessed name.
Leader: Idiots make every attempt to evade giving honor to the name of God.
People: Yet, without words, the name is spoken through the star spangled heavens.
Leader: Without articulation the name blazes in sunrises and sunsets.
People: The breeze through the trees echoes the name.
Leader: The tiny, fragile flower, pushing its way through concrete, shouts out the name.
People: Then, we look in the eyes of infants and those who are aging with grace and the matchless name is whispered again.
All: For God's name is a household word.

Benediction

Leader: The Lord bless you and keep you.
People: The Lord's face shine upon you.
Leader: The Lord be gracious unto you.
People: The countenance of the Lord be lifted upon you.
Leader: May the Lord, our God, grant you great shalom! Amen.
People: Hallelujah and amen.

4 · The Season of Epiphany

The Greco-Roman world gave us the word *epiphany*. Epiphany designated for them the occasion when state officials made public appearances within the provinces. The early Church adopted the term to indicate the manifestations of Christ within the world. During Epiphany we get different snapshots of the Savior's brilliant glory.

The Greek word *epiphaneia* means to manifest, show forth, or make clear. The bright star of Bethlehem guided the Wise to get a glimpse of the newborn Sovereign. During this season of illumination, many sightings of the Divine will help us view the many-faceted aspects of our great Savior and the plan for our salvation.

January 6 is the official Feast of Epiphany. This date signals the arrival of the known world to give honor and treasure to Jesus and also signifies his baptism by John when the full Trinity is displayed.

The intent of the month of January in general is new beginnings, fresh starts, and the additional opportunities God supplies for us. Its theme can be the light of justice. Epiphany, baptismal renewal, and the Dr. Martin Luther King, Jr. celebration are priorities of this month.

Altar Focus

To symbolize light, a large, old-fashioned kerosene lamp can be the altar focus for the first Sunday in January. A menorah, with black, red, and green candles, can be placed between the usual Christ candles. When Epiphany is celebrated on the Sunday nearest January 6, the altar focus can feature water pitchers of various shapes and sizes, goblets, crystal decanters, and treasure chests. This is another liturgical day of white, and gold stars will enhance the world "illumination."

On the Sunday that reaffirmation of baptism is celebrated, a large, clear, crystal bowl filled with water or one of the "heritage" wash basins and pitchers, can be featured. Conch shells, dried sponges, and assorted sea shells call out, "Take me to the water!"[18] The baptismal font and other symbols of baptism are welcomed. The Sunday nearest January 6 is the opportune day for celebrating baptismal renewal.

For Dr. King's celebration, a grapevine wreath may be the altar focus, wrapped in black, red, and green cloth or paper, with large red flowers having yellow centers, to represent our homeland and our continuing struggle for liberty and justice. The altar need not be fully changed weekly, but enhanced for the particular liturgical setting of worship.

EPIPHANY

Isaiah 60:1–6
Psalm 72:1–14
Ephesians 3:1–12
Matthew 2:1–12

Call to Worship

Leader: Have you not heard? Did you not know? Christ went to Africa!
People: What in the world do you mean?
Leader: God sent the Light of the World to Africa!
People: Why did this happen?
Leader: The spirit of death was seeking to extinguish the Light. Africa was hospitable and welcomed her son home.
People: Let's give the Radiant God praise for a goodly land that provided refuge for the Hope of the World!

Responsive Reading Psalm 72

Leader: Warrior God, we praise you for the reign of your son.
People: He came to judge the poor with justice and your inheritance with righteousness.
Leader: We continue to pray that Jesus Christ will defeat our foes, root out systems of poverty, and send us deliverance from every oppressor.
People: Jesus, our elder brother, has lived among us since the generations of the ancestors.
Leader: May his loving ways be like fresh rain, which showers the earth and her inhabitants.
People: Our hearts long for his reign of right living and abiding peace.
Leader: May the world's leaders render their hearts to his leading. May the rulers of every province and tribe bring the sacrifice of their willing spirit. May the wealthy and the greedy bow before him in reverence and in honor.
People: For their hearts are yet in God's hands. And without God we have no help.
Leader: But we have received mercy from God in our past.

People: From oppression and violence, God has redeemed our life. Those who have died, struggling for justice, are precious in the sight of our God.
Unison: God preserves the lives of those who are in need!

Call to Confession

The Light has come and too often we refuse to acknowledge its presence. Let us confess our preference for the absence of illumination.

Confession

Lord of light and ability to see, we confess our sin of ignoring you and refusing to open our eyes to your radiance. Your light causes us to look inward to change, and not outward to blame others. Your light pulls us up to action instead of down in hopelessness. Your light means transformation and change. Your light scares us! Forgive us, we pray, for our sin.

Words of Assurance

Lift up your eyes and look around; the glory of the Lord shines on you and in you! Your sons and your daughters shall see and be radiant! Your heart shall thrill and rejoice, because abundance and the wealth of nations shall come to you. Praise the Lord!

Offertory Invitation

The wise of every generation know to open their treasures to the Inspiration of Glory. The Wise offered what they had. This privilege is ours today.

Offertory Praise

Jesus Christ came and opened his treasure chest of inheritance unto us. Now we have access to God and boldness and confidence through faith in him. So that the world might know this birthright, we offer what is ours. In the name of the Giver, we pray.

Benediction

Leader: The star is yet shining and people are yet looking for the Light of the World!
People: We leave to point the way.
Leader: The manger is empty, and the angelic choir no longer sings.
People: Christ is at home in our hearts! His song of victory is on our lips.
Leader: The light of Christ will lead you, the love of Christ will enfold you, and the spirit of Christ will live through you, world without end! Amen and amen!

THE FIRST SUNDAY AFTER EPIPHANY
BAPTISMAL/COVENANT RENEWAL

Isaiah 42:1–9
Psalm 29
Acts 10:34–43
Matthew 3:13–17

Call to Worship

Leader: We gather to worship the Living Water!
People: Spring up, Oh Well, within our souls.[19]
Leader: In our dry and arid places, Water of Baptism, refresh us.
People: Bubble up, Living Water, renew us.
Leader: The baptism of the Ethiopian official of Candace, sovereign queen of Ethiopia, remind us of our connection to both the first Church and the Eternal Well, which never runs dry.
People: Gush within us, overflow us to saturate the stagnant areas of our lives, and reconnect us to our Source.
Leader: Let's remember our baptism and be thankful!
People: Take us to the waters! Let's renew our baptismal vows. Amen.

Call to Confession

How often we forget or neglect our covenant and baptismal vows. We live like those who have no obligations or responsibilities. Let's confess our sin.

Confession

Covenant God, you made us your people and gave your Son as a pledge of your love. It was by his blood that we were baptized into relationship with you. Yet, we make trivial both his blood and the water, which symbolizes our entry into the Church. Forgive us our sin. Restore us to harmony with you, we pray.

Words of Assurance

Truly, God shows no partiality but, in every nation, anyone who will give God reverence and do the right thing is acceptable. Thanks be to God!

Responsive Reading Isaiah 42:1–9

Leader: Jesus was the Suffering Servant, chosen by God, born of Mary, and baptized by John.

People: The Holy Spirit rested upon him and God thundered from the heavens, for baptism is a family affair.

Leader: Through the baptism, ministry, death, and resurrection of Jesus, justice has been seen by every nation.

People: He did not whine or yell; the macho image was not his choice. He never resorted to violence but worked faithfully to model and teach justice and equality.

Leader: His spirit is alive in us today. We cannot grow faint, we will not be crushed until the reign of Christ is established throughout the earth.

People: The Lord of Hosts, Creator of heaven and earth, has called us to right living, taken us by our feeble hands, given strength to our knees, and kept us till this day.

Leader: You are a covenant, a light, the vision to prisoners, yet enslaved.

People: Steadfast is our God. We offer God praise and glory. For the promises of God have been faithful and true.

Unison: The Lord strengthens us. The Lord blesses us with shalom!

Offertory Invitation

The covenant was initiated by the God of all. Whatever we give is a gift we have already received. Give from a grateful heart!

Offertory Praise

The voice of the Lord is over the waters; the God of glory thunders and we worship the Lord; in holy splendor, with our giving.

Benediction

Leader: Once again we have been refreshed with baptismal waters.

People: Let it be so now; for it is proper for us, in this way, to fulfill all righteousness.

Leader: The heavens are opened to you, the Holy Spirit is available to you, and God affirms, "You are my beloved, well-pleasing in my sight!"

People: May it always be so! Amen.

THE SECOND SUNDAY AFTER EPIPHANY
DR. MARTIN L. KING, JR. SUNDAY

Isaiah 49:1–7
Psalm 40:1–11
I Corinthians 1:1–9
John 1:29–42

Call to Worship

Leader: The God of dreamers and visionaries summons us!
People: I have a dream![20]
Leader: The God who works in us the will and the ability to live, work, and die for justice, is in our midst.
People: I have a dream!
Leader: The God who speaks to us in dreams and reveals mystery to us in visions demands our attention!
People: I have a dream!
Leader: Before you were born, while yet in your mother's womb, God formed you and called you by name.
People: I am a dream! Thanks be to God!

Call to Confession

Too often we have relegated dreams to be only the source of the numbers runner or the lotto! But God speaks in the complexity of our dreaming. Let us confess our failure to respond.

Confession

God of dreams and dreamers, forgive us for being so casual with your revelation knowledge. Instead of heeding your messages for our lives, we have envisioned only big cars, huge houses, and vacation escapes abroad! Trying so hard to escape our poverty, we have missed your signs and symbols of authentic life. Forgive us our sin. Help us to dream of better and different tomorrows. Help us to work diligently for justice. And help us to act justly in all of our dealings. In the name of the Vision of Hope, we pray.

Words of Assurance

Sisters and brothers, you know what is right and what God requires. It is that we do justice, love kindness, and walk dependent upon God. This is made possible by the Holy Spirit, who lives and reigns in you. Glory to God!

Responsive Reading Psalm 40

Leader: We have waited, sometimes not so patiently, for the Lord. Many times it has seemed as if God did not know our names, nor hear our petitions!

People: Yet, from slave ships, slavery, Jim Crow, and "unseen" lynchings we have been delivered. These were horrible and desolate pits and God was our Rock of Security.

Leader: The '60s, with civil rights, voting rights, and the death of "formal" segregation, gave us a brand new song. "We shall overcome!"[21] became our praise unto God!

People: Many around the world saw our deliverance and put their trust in our God. The people at the wall of Berlin, the students in Tiananmen Square, the workers of Poland, and our siblings in South Africa made the God of justice theirs!

Leader: Those who dare wait on divine time, who do not give over to their victim status, and who refuse to believe in the false gods of greed and oppression will be blessed!

People: Despite being treated unjustly, denied basic human rights or the agreed-upon restitution, "forty acres and a mule," God has multiplied us and brought us this far by faith.

Leader: Our God is wondrous; there is none like our Sovereign. The thoughts of God toward us are more in number than grains of sand.

People: The sacrifice of our own blood is not always required, but a willingness to follow after God with our whole heart is absolutely necessary.

Leader: Many brave sisters and brothers have sacrificed their lives on our behalf. Today, we recall the life and ministry of Dr. Martin Luther King, Jr., who said to God, "Here I am! I delight to do your will. Oh, God, your law is within my heart!"

People: When mother Rosa Parks sat down, the God in Dr. Martin Luther King, Jr. stood up to tell the glad news of deliverance in the great congregation.

Leader: The saving help of our God is continually spoken of and the steadfast love of the Lord is our salvation.

People: God, do not withhold your mercy from us. Raise us up to do our part in the fight for justice. Let your love and faithfulness call us to greater service forever!

Offertory Invitation

God is faithful! Through the gift of God we have been called into this fellowship with Jesus Christ. Let us share our gifts in order to spread this good news!

Offertory Praise

Jesus called us to "Come and see." Use these, our gifts, in order that we may participate in the "go and tell" of helping others find the Christ. Amen.

Benediction

Leader: Go! In the spirit of Dr. Martin Luther King, Jr., who had a dream and lived for it.

People: Thank God for dreams and dreamers.

Leader: Go! In the spirit of mother Rosa Parks, who had a vision of equality and justice and lives for it.

People: Thank the Proclaimer of Justice for visions and visionaries.

Leader: Thank God for the spirit of justice, alive and spreading throughout the world.

People: Thank the Redeemer of the oppressed for another opportunity to have a dream, see a vision, and be a justice seeker!

Leader: Go! In the power of the Achievable God! Amen and amen!

THE THIRD SUNDAY AFTER EPIPHANY

Isaiah 9:1–4
Psalm 27:1–9
I Corinthians 1:10–18
Matthew 4:12–23

Call to Worship

Leader: Welcome to the hospital of the saints!
People: What do you mean, hospital? We have come to church!
Leader: The anguished and brokenhearted have a place in this sanctuary. There is a balm in Gilead![22]
People: Our spirits are wounded, sometimes we are in pain, but we have on our "church faces!"
Leader: Take them off! Cast them aside! The healing God is present to lift burdens, bind wounds, and mend broken hearts. Rejoice and prepare for worship.
People: Alleluia! Praise to Zion's Anointed!

Call to Confession

The promise of Isaiah is that there will be no gloom for those who are in anguish! We have become comfortable living in contempt and pain. Let us confess our need for healing and restoration.

Confession

Incomparable Christ, you called us to follow. Yet, we sensed there would be pain and lingered afar off. You said, "Follow me and I will make you fishers of souls." But too many people have mistreated us, hurt us, and killed us, until we are just not ready to reach out to them. So our hearts have hardened, our ears have closed, and our mouths have remained shut to repentance. But we desire to be made whole. Forgive us, heal us, and help us to follow you. Amen.

Words of Assurance

To all who have sat in gloom, the Light has come. It is a healing Light! Rejoice and be glad, for your yokes are destroyed. Amen.

Responsive Reading Psalm 27

Leader: The Lord is our health and our wholeness; no longer will fear and anxiety make us sick!
People: The Lord is the security of our life; we have no reason to be afraid.
Leader: We have one common petition before the Lord, and we will hold onto the horns of the altar until our requests are granted.
People: We want unity among our people. We want to reflect the beauty of the Lord in our wide array of colors, and we want to appreciate the vast richness of our history.
Leader: God has lifted us in spite of our enemies all around. In this place we will give shouts of joy! We will lift our voices in songs of praise.
People: Hearing God, answer when we call! Be gracious, is our plea.
Leader: Our hearts say, "Come, Lord." We long to see your face.
People: Even in our hostility and rebellion, do not turn away in anger. You have been our help in ages past. Don't leave us alone. Only you can provide the healing and wholeness that we need.

Offertory Invitation

There is no charge for the healing. The oil of anointing flows freely. In order that the doors of healing stations may remain open around the world, let us share our resources.

Offertory Praise

Wounded Healer, we give you praise for the opportunity to participate in spreading wholeness throughout the world. In the name of the Bearer of Scars, we pray.

Benediction

Leader: Jesus went throughout the land, teaching, proclaiming good news, and curing every disease and sickness among the people. Go! Do the same, in his power and with his authority!
People: Amen!

THE FOURTH SUNDAY AFTER EPIPHANY

Micah 6:1–8
Psalm 15
I Corinthians 1:18–31
Matthew 5:1–12

Call to Worship

Leader: The Righteous Judge has called us to order.
People: We have come to give witness this morning.
Leader: Plead your case before the Ultimate Law. Your controversy against goodness will be heard.
People: We know what justice demands of us—we are to love compassion and to be companions with temperance and self-control. The Court wins.
Leader: The Chief Magistrate ruled in your favor at Calvary!
People: Thank God for Jesus, the Lawyer who has never lost a case! We come to offer our praise and worship. Amen.

Call to Confession

The torture stake, planted high on a garbage dump, seems foolish if you don't know the end of the story. An unjust killing seems biased toward wrong if you don't know the results of that death. We think we are wise. We think we can debate with the plan that has already worked. We try to remove the blood from Calvary and make it nice and neat. Our wisdom has resulted in sin. Let us confess.

Confession

Wisdom of the Ages, we recognize that your folly is well planned on our behalf. We comprehend that your frailty is deliberate and more strong than our human force. Thank you for revealing your love by dying, that we might live. Thank you for becoming poor, that we might inherit everything. We have been absurd in our rational thinking and have sinned against you. Forgive us our sin. We cannot boast in your presence. Restore us to joyful relationship with you, we pray. Amen.

Words of Assurance

Jesus Christ is our life in God! Jesus Christ died that we might become wise. It was in the death of Jesus Christ that our right standing, salvation, and liberation were secured. We can boast in our life in Christ. Thanks be unto God. Amen.

Responsive Reading Psalm 15

Leader: Who may enter the house of holiness? Who may remain in the presence of Pure Power?
People: Those sick of violence and decay, those filled with loving deeds and those whose mouths issue words of truth are welcomed to the Heart of Heaven's Best.
Leader: Evil wants to reign in us. Outrage raises its voice within us. And there is the noise of fury all around.
People: Yet, our battle cry is "Peace." Our weapon is love. And our power is in prayer.
Leader: The world will despise you. Lies will continue to pass as truth.
People: We will honor the Ancient of Days with our lives, with both our words and deeds. We will respect the dignity of each one and honor each as a child of the Most High.
Leader: If you practice what you have learned, nothing can separate you from everlasting life.

Offertory Invitation

The blessings of God have made us wealthy in every manner. Out of our abundant storage, let us share.

Offertory Praise

God of all, to you we raise these our gifts of gratefulness and thanks. Our dependence is upon you. From what you have given, we offer a just portion for use in spreading your realm. Amen.

Benediction

Leader: Joyous are those whose spirits yearn for harmony with the world.
People: Heaven belongs to them.
Leader: Happy are those who shed emotional tears.
People: Comfort is promised.
Leader: Content are those who depend upon God.

People: A place of peace is theirs.

Leader: Glad are those with appetites for the right.

People: They will be satisfied.

Leader: Ecstatic are those who provide grace in difficult times.

People: Good will always find them.

Leader: In a hate-filled world, peacemakers are sought.

People: These are the children of God.

Leader: Exhilaration is the watchword for those who have suffered violence and wrath.

People: We have been reviled and persecuted and have faced all types of evil, falsely.

Leader: Go with great joy! The Potentate of Paradise, the Christ of Calvary, and the inspiration of the Holy Spirit go before us! Amen.

THE FIFTH SUNDAY AFTER EPIPHANY

Isaiah 58:1–12
Psalm 112:1–10
I Corinthians 2:1–16
Matthew 5:13–20

Call to Worship

Leader: The Communicator of love, joy, and grace has called!

People: We have received this communication with gladness. Nothing can separate us from God's unchanging love.

Leader: In our confusion, our anxiety, and even our brokenness, we are surrounded by God's love and care.

People: We feel the welcome of the Nurturing God. In this sacred space, we will be renewed.

Leader: This is God's house! It is a place of restoration, filled with the Son's radiance. It is open for you.

People: We have answered the call to come and worship the Lord!

Call to Confession

Shout out, do not hold back! Lift up your voice like a trumpet! Let us recognize and acknowledge our rebellion against the call of Love. Let's confess our sin.

Confession

Cry of the longing heart, hope of the repentant, hear the confession of our lips and respond to the speech of our silence. We know how we have hurt you, grieved you, and caused you pain by our turning away. We have forsaken your laws and have not practiced right living. But we turn to you. Forgive us our sin and restore us to a place of delight in your realm. We ask in the name of the Keeper of our souls. Amen.

Words of Assurance

The Vindicator has gone before us to prepare the way. When we earnestly repent, our light shall break forth as the dawn, and our healing shall spring up quickly. When we call, the Ancient of Days will answer our cry for help and respond, "Here I am!" Thanks be to God!

Responsive Reading Psalm 112:1–10

Leader: Praise the Answer of all mysteries! Those who give reverence and delight in doing God's commandments already live in the circle of divine care.

People: In spite of what we see and what the media reports, God has promised to uphold and to preserve our children and even their posterity.

Leader: Poverty, unemployment, and economic deprivation are present all around us, yet we are wealthy and possess a vast inheritance. The legacy of our people will endure forever.

People: It is amazing to the world that we sing, laugh, rejoice, and give praise in difficulty. They cannot comprehend how we can continue to be gracious, merciful, and faith-filled when evil is so pervasive.

Leader: But the foreparents taught us that "If you live right, heaven belongs to you!" And heaven is not some far-away place!

People: We have learned not to fear evil or evildoers. The myth that we will become extinct goes against our history. The pages of eternity tell our story!

Leader: Our hearts are set on the Living Word, who stirs us and gives us our hope. We rock steady, while others stumble and fall. It is written that we will triumph!

People: We will continue sharing what we have, helping the less fortunate among us, welcoming the stranger and extending ourselves for each other. Our oil and meal will never run out, for the Bread of Life is among us!

Leader: The wicked see it and get angry. They plot and plan, but it is in vain. Their desires come to nothing!

People: We give praise to the Answer of all mysteries! Amen!

Offertory Invitation

No eye has seen, no ear has ever heard, and no human heart can ever conceive what the Provider of All has in store for those who love and give out of that love. It is a real mystery why God bestows so lavishly on us! Let us share out of a sense of thankfulness.

Offertory Praise

Lavishly Generous One, how we adore you for the opportunity to sow into your spiritual mysteries. Receive now our gifts and use them to spread your love and care.

Benediction

Leader: You are the salt of the earth!
People: We will preserve God's Word in our hearts.
Leader: You are the lights of the world!
People: We will not hide our distinct flavor from our neighbors or friends.
Leader: Do good deeds, but give God the glory for them.
People: We have been given the mind of Christ, which calls us, not to mere words, but to loving action!
Leader: The Communicator of Love goes before you, to keep you and to preserve you in all you say and do! Amen!

Doxology for Black History Month

Praise God, ye dark ones of the land
Sing praise for the Ancient's sustaining hand
For all these gifts we have to share
Sing praise for God's blessings everywhere!

Song of the Month

"Lift Every Voice and Sing!"[23]

THE SIXTH SUNDAY AFTER EPIPHANY

Deuteronomy 30:15–20
Psalm 119:1–8
I Corinthians 3:1–9
Matthew 5:21–37

Call to Worship

Leader: Choose life that you and your children may live!
People: But violence is rampant in our communities.
Leader: Let righteousness and faithfulness be your aim!
People: But our children are killing each other and us!
Leader: Let reconciliation be the goal of every relationship.
People: We gather with upright hearts to worship the God of promise and hope!

Call to Confession

So often the chaos of our lives prevents us from being steadfast in our focus on the Healing God. Let us confess our sin.

Confession

The lure of "don't worry, be happy"[24] has pulled us away from the God of struggle. Our feet have failed to follow the straight paths, our tongues have engaged in half truths and lies, and our hearts have grown cold to the narrow way. Yet we want to choose life! Forgive us our debts and place our sin in the sea of forgetfulness. Then help us to forgive ourselves. In the name of Truth, we pray. Amen.

Words of Assurance

Reconciliation began with God's promise to Eve that her seed would bring forth death to evil. Forgiveness, healing, and restoration are ours because of Calvary. This is mighty good news!

Responsive Reading Psalm 119:1–7, 165

Leader: When we walk with the illumination received from the Logos, it becomes alive in us and we are blessed to be blessings!

People: Contentment reigns in our hearts because we know that God's promises are always true. Despite present situations, our history evidences God's faithfulness.

Leader: We can follow a trustworthy God and walk in confidence.

People: The Parent God is stern, requiring diligence to every precept and commandment, which are for the keeping of our souls.

Leader: Oh, that our lives might conform to the ways of God.

People: We will never be made ashamed!

Leader: With made-up minds we can learn to be people of God.

People: Steadfast love will not forsake us in our efforts. Great peace belongs to those who will observe God's law. No evil can make us stumble or fall.

Offertory Invitation

One plants, another waters, but it is God who causes growth. Each one who plants and waters has a common purpose, to work with the God of harvest. As God's servants, let us work together to bring about a new realm.

Offertory Praise

Reconciling and Healing God, we bring our gifts to the altar as a sign that we are in right relationship with our brothers and sisters in the world. Use these gifts for your great purpose of extending life and love.

Benediction

Leader: The God of the ancestors bless you.

People: The Ancient of Days enfold you.

Leader: The Light of Glory shine upon you.

People: The Darkness of Growth give you sound sleep.

Leader: The Help of the Ages goes with us.

People: The Hope of Tomorrow bids us, "Come."

Leader: Let's leave, to walk in this faith! Amen!

THE SEVENTH SUNDAY AFTER EPIPHANY

Leviticus 19:1–2, 9–18
Psalm 119:33–40
1 Corinthians 3:10–23
Matthew 5:38–48

Call to Worship

Leader: The Lord of Hosts spoke to Moses and the congregation.
People: God's word was, "You shall be holy, for I, your God, am holy."
Leader: Holiness is a high standard to reach.
People: But, in our worship, it is God who reaches for us!
Leader: Let us worship the Beauty of Holiness with praise.

Call to Confession

Because the standards of God are so exacting, often we feel they are impossible to reach, and we stop trying. Let's confess our sin before the God who called us.

Confession

God, we recognize in our heads that our bodies are your temple and that you have sent the Holy Spirit to live in us, to lead us, and guide us into your truth and ways. But so often it is easier to be the captains of our own ships and the masters of our own fate. We refuse to acknowledge you and listen to those whose standards are easier to maintain. We acknowledge that you know our foolishness. We want to belong to you and to have you be pleased with our lives. Forgive us our sin. Amen.

Words of Assurance

Confession means that we are God's dwelling and all things of God belong to us. The things of this world, in life and in death—even the future belongs to us! For we belong to Christ and Christ belongs to God! Amen.

Responsive Reading Psalm 119:33–40, 165

Leader: The Maker of beauty taught the ancestors the way in the lush tropics of Africa. These laws traveled with us in our collective consciousness.

People: God, grant us understanding of your many promises and precepts so that we can follow your way with our whole hearts.

Leader: Like the ancestors were led through the Middle Passage, having internal knowledge of God's will, we seek that conviction for our lives today.

People: Fix your way firmly in our hearts so that nothing done to us causes us to forget nor look away.

Leader: Help us not to find the prosperity of the oppressor attractive, but lead us to ways of abundant life.

People: Show us further evidences of your confirming promises in our lives so that our faith is made stronger yet.

Leader: We know that your way is better, but we hate being scorned and despised. Take away our disgrace; give us renewed dignity.

People: In your word there is life. Help us to see the reality of your promise that "Great peace have they which love your law and nothing can make them stumble!"

Offertory Invitation

According to the grace that God has given unto us, like a skilled builder, with our sharing we lay a foundation. We must each choose with care how to build upon this foundation. Returning to God a portion of our means makes the work of ministry more firm.

Offertory Praise

Jesus Christ, you are our foundation. We give you thanks for the security of our faith. May these offerings be used to spread the building of your realm in the world.

Benediction

Leader: Leave knowing that the Lord of the harvest goes before you.

People: We must not steal, deal falsely with each other, or lie to one another.

Leader: You shall not swear falsely, profane the name of God, or deceive your neighbors.

People: We will not put stumbling blocks in the way or give judgements that are unjust. We will care for the poor and speak out for the oppressed.

Leader: Do not hate anyone or bear grudges. Leave to be the Church!

People: We leave with the love of God, going out to love our neighbors as we love ourselves! Amen!

THE EIGHTH SUNDAY AFTER EPIPHANY

Isaiah 49:8–16a
Psalm 131
1 Corinthians 4:1–5
Matthew 6:24–34

Call to Worship

Leader: The Comforter of Zion is present!
People: Our hearts are heavy; our pain is great!
Leader: The Compassionate One is in our midst.
People: Our tears are many; our laughter is almost stilled.
Leader: Come ye, disconsolate,[25] bring your sorrows and cares. The Weeping God awaits your company!
People: God is our Rock in a weary land![26] God is our shelter from life's storms. We worship the God of comfort, compassion, and care!

Call to Confession

Sometimes the cares of life weigh us down so, until we forget that God is concerned and involved in every facet of our lives. Let us confess our sin, which separates us from divine comfort.

Confession

Wisdom of the ages, we turn to you in repentance. In times of favor and good fortune, we remember you. On the good days, we tell of your salvation. But the daily news, economic forecasts, and political climate in our world cause our attention to wander from you. Forgive us for doubting your ability to pull high places down and lift the lowly. Consoler of the penitent, restore, renew, and refresh us, is our prayer.

Words of Assurance

The God of Zion cannot forget us! The promise declares, "Can a mother forget her nursing child, or show no compassion for the child of her womb?" Even these may forget, yet I will not! I have you inscribed in the palm of my hand! This is the good news!

Responsive Reading The Community's Lament (Psalm 86)

Leader: All-seeing, all-knowing God, our tears are before you day and night. Heed our petitions, answer when we cry.

People: Our spirit is troubled; we are weighed down with grief. Oft times we feel that we do not matter to you, that we are invisible and inconsequential in the world.

Leader: The issue of abandonment is ever painful for us. And when we seek your interventions and cannot see your face, we are simply overwhelmed.

People: Have you counted us as insignificant? Is our status as so-called minorities and our dark coloring of no matter to even you? You made us, you called us, we have gathered in your name. We are here—but where are you?

Leader: There is nothing solid about our existence. Chaos and confusion are everywhere. When we feel we have made a significant gain, we are pushed further back in other areas of life. We call out to you and you do not answer! We cry, and your comfort is not!

People: We seek your pity and even you are counted among the indifferent! Is your Word really true? Is your counsel available? Do you honestly provide a balm for broken hearts and wounded spirits?

Leader: We are exhausted with trying—trying to do your will, trying to remain faithful, trying to see possibilities in the world's madness, trying to sing when the melody is gone, trying not to tell a story that is filled with an evil world and an absent God!

People: We lift our hands, and our arms are like lead. We open our mouths, and our tongues are like brass. We want to open our hearts, but the pain of rejection lingers so long! We want to believe in the Church, but where is the salvation for the neglected and the forgotten?

Leader: "Why us?" we cry, and there is no response. "How much more?" we inquire, and another blow slams us against the wall. "How long?" we beg, and the silence mocks us!

People: And yet we stand. Waiting. Seeking. Longing. We know you have come before on behalf of the oppressed. You are the God who comes! So we will wait for you!

Offertory Invitation

As servants of Christ and stewards of God's mysteries, it is required of us to be trustworthy in our returning a just portion of what we have received.

Offertory Praise

God of Abundance, we are devoted to your service. Your care of birds and lilies, who do not work, pledge, or tithe, is a constant reminder of your generosity to us. May our gifts be a symbol of our thanksgiving. Use them to bless your work in the world.

Benediction

Leader: Your life is in God's capable hands.
People: There is a balm in Gilead.[27]
Leader: The Restorer of ruptures goes before you.
People: Healing belongs to the people of God.
Leader: Do not worry about tomorrow, God knows your every need.
People: We can return to the world with confidence.
Leader: When you seek the realm of shalom it comes to dwell in you and to work through you.
People: We will carry the shalom of Zion wherever we go!

THE NINTH SUNDAY AFTER EPIPHANY

Deuteronomy 11:18–28
Psalm 31:1–5, 19–24
Romans 1:16–31
Matthew 7:21–29

Call to Worship

Leader: We gather that the Word of life might encourage and enrich our hearts.

People: We come that our children might learn of God's intervention in our lives.

Leader: We assemble to rehearse our faith story, to name our heroes and heroines, and to give praise and worship to the Eternal.

People: The God of the diaspora, black, dark, and silent, is worthy of our worship and our praise.

Call to Confession

In our humanness, we forget our unique call and purpose in life. Allow your spirits to rise in confession before the Ancient of Days.

Confession

God of technicolor people, forgive us for being ashamed of our "isness" in you. Too often we curse ourselves, instead of remembering your saving acts throughout our history. Forgive our sin and help us to embrace the blessings of our lives.

Words of Assurance

Jesus is the Light of the world[28] and that Light shines through us when we turn in repentance and openness with our confession. The words of our mouths and the meditations of our hearts give us reconciliation with God.

Responsive Reading Psalm 31

Leader: Precious Lord, take our hands, lead us on, let us stand![29] We seek our refuge in you. Our color has been a badge of shame. Our history has

been made into a patchwork quilt of lies and myths. In your righteousness deliver us.

People: Hear our cries. Answer our calls. Hold our hands, lest we fall.[30]
Send us speedy deliverance. Be our strong tower in these shifting times.

Leader: Name above all names, help us to escape the evil plots and racist
plans that threaten us on every side. Helper of ages past, we hide our
hope in you.

People: Spirit of the ancestors, you have been faithful. For the matriarchs
and patriarchs who have taught us about your redemption, we give you
praise. Because of their faith stories, we rely upon you and commit our
lives into your saving hands.

Leader: Great is your faithfulness toward all who love you. The roll call of
our saints is tremendous. From the Gold Coast of Africa, through the
cotton fields of the south, in the great migration north and the industrial
call of the Midwest, the names and deeds of those who have lived and
died for justice are legion!

People: Phyllis Wheaties, poet; Harriet Tubman, black liberator;
Sojourner Truth, preacher of freedom; Mary McClod Bethune, educator;
Mary Church Terrell, organizer; Rosa Parks, mother of the civil rights
movement; Coretta Scott King, keeper of the dream; and Betty Shabazz,
queen of dignity, are among those who dwell in you with safety.

Leader: Aesop, writer of fables; Tertullian, theologian; Saints Cyprian
and Augustine; Crispus Attucks, warrior; Marcus Garvey, organizer;
Jomo Kenyatta, Kenya's first prime minister; Richard Wright, author;
Claude McKay, writer-poet; Lerone Bennett, historian; and Benjamin E.
Mays, philosopher, all set the stage for Martin, Malcolm, and Megar to
be used in your divine plan of justice.

People: In the shelter of your presence, hide them. In the security of your
love, hold them close.

Leader: We will bless the Trumpet of Zion, who has been steadfast in
every phase of our journey.

People: In our most fearful times, we feel God is absent and that we are
invisible. Yet it is evident that God has always heard our cries.

Leader: Saints, love God! We have been preserved!

People: Our hearts take courage and we are strengthened as we continue
to wait on the Salvation of Zion!

Offertory Invitation

We are not ashamed of this good news; it is the power of God for deliverance to everyone who believes. In faithfulness, let us share our gifts.

Offertory Praise

God, all of us have sinned and fallen short of your glory. Yet you gave us Jesus, a gift of grace. Receive now our gifts and use them to your continuing glory and praise.

Benediction:

Leader: Saint Cyprian instructs us:
People: "Every age is reminded by what it hears, that what has been done, can be done again!"[31]
Leader: Harriet Tubman challenges us:
People: ". . . there was one of two things, I had a right to liberty or death. . . . I should fight for my liberty as long as my strength lasts."[32]
Leader: Charlotte Forten blesses us:
People: "Dear children, born in slavery, but free at last! May God preserve to you all the blessings of freedom and may you be in every possible way fitted to enjoy them."[33]
Leader: Therefore, go into the world, with the love of God, the intercession of God's Son, and the power of the Holy Spirit, living the words of Dr. Martin Luther King, Jr.
Unison: "We must use time creatively . . . and forever realize that time is always ripe for us to do right!"[34] Amen!

THE LAST SUNDAY AFTER EPIPHANY

TRANSFIGURATION SUNDAY
Exodus 24:12–18
Psalm 2
2 Peter 1:16–21
Matthew 17:1–9

Call to Worship

Leader: Arise! Shine! For the Light has come!
People: How brilliant and glorious is our God!
Leader: Arise! Shine! For the Light is here!
People: The Awesome God commands our attention!
Leader: Arise! Shine! Let's worship God in the beauty of holiness!

Call to Confession

The God of the Mountains calls us to come to the high places. Yet we prefer to dwell in the low plains and surrender to lesser gods. Let's confess our sin.

Confession

Incomparable One, we confess our sin. We follow our own devious myths; we listen to our own interpretations; and we refuse to heed your invitation to climb the mountain and dwell in your presence. Forgive us. We pray in the name of Christ. Amen.

Words of Assurance

Confession leads us back to right relationship with a loving and forgiving God. Indeed, this is good news!

Responsive Reading Psalm 2

Leader: It's the same old story! Dark-skinned people around the globe continue to be mistreated, cast aside, and conspired against by those in power.
People: Why do entire nations scheme against us? What makes hate groups continue to devise methods for our eradication?

Leader: We are continually removed from power centers, forced to work for the lowest possible pay, stripped of political influence through redlining and gerrymandering, viewed and regarded as subhuman, while we are the people who possess the secret of joy!

People: The God of many deliverances laughs at the oppressors. In wrath and fury the vengeance of God will be unleashed against them.

Leader: The Friend of Zion has come and identified with the marginal and oppressed.

People: The Chosen of God is in Zion! We have been established as the salt of the earth, the light of the world, a nation that cannot be hidden.

Leader: The nations of the earth sprang forth from our loins. The ends of the earth belong to us. Poverty shall be broken and injustice will crumble like a potter's vessel.

People: When we come into power, let wisdom work perfectly in us. We will serve the First and Last with awe. Our hope and our wholeness is complete in God!

Offertory Invitation

A new day dawns! Let the Morning Star shine through giving. As we have witnessed God's majesty and glory, we are called to enable in others this same opportunity.

Offertory Praise

Transfigured Savior, we have seen your glory and been drawn to the high places. Use our gifts so that your face may shine around the world.

Benediction

Leader: We cannot make a permanent dwelling in this place!

People: But here we are safe and secure from all alarms!

Leader: You have heard God's voice, calling you "beloved."

People: We have felt an empowering touch and we are more whole.

Leader: Go out, wrapped in the Glory, bedazzled by the Vision, and reassured by the Holy Presence. Tell the story and be a witness! Amen.

5 · The Season of Lent

We become pilgrims on a forty-day journey, seeking our way out of the wilderness of sin in the season of Lent. It is a serious period of spiritual discipline as we either give up something pleasant or take on a new mission to enable others. Lent is our individual struggle to subdue our flesh and to wrestle with the sin issue, which tempts us so readily.

The early church prepared new members, catechumens, for Easter Sunday baptism. There was an intense year of being indoctrinated into the faith community. Both instructors and students of the faith fasted, prayed, studied, and made themselves more consciously aware of the sacrifice of Jesus Christ.

The Israelites wandered forty years in the wilderness. Jesus spent forty days and nights struggling with Satan in the wilderness. We will journey through our own forty-day wilderness, knowing that resurrection is on the way.

It is good to note that Sundays are not included in the forty-day Lenten period. For each Sunday worship experience is a reenactment of the resurrection!

Altar Focus

As the drama of Lent unfolds, with its journey toward the cross and resurrection, the altar should set a tempo for meditation and reflection. A Lenten garden might be a possibility for you. Local florists will gather the necessary plants and rent them for the season. Included should be any plant that will remind us of the Garden of Gethsemane, the place where Jesus spent his hours anticipating death for us.

Stalks of wheat and vines should be heavily emphasized as Jesus is the Bread of Life and the Vine from which we are nourished. Wheat was most likely the most important cultivated crop in that period. A huge rock or simulated boulder should be included to remind us of wise and foolish persons who select to build their faith on rock or sand. Perhaps a quiet waterfall might be included so that your altar would attract members during the weeks ahead, as a sacred spot for stopping to take a drink from the Fountain of Life, which never runs dry. Let your imagination flow and allow the artistry of your worship committee to make the garden one to remember. If you place lilies around the altar the day before Easter, the beauty will be striking!

This period of the church's year also includes Women's History Month in March. International Women's History Day is March 8. You will find a focus on the contributions of women throughout the liturgies.

ASH WEDNESDAY

Joel 2:1–17
Psalm 51:1–17
2 Corinthians 5:20–6:10
Matthew 6:1–21

Call to Worship

Leader: Blow the trumpet in Zion! Sound the alarm!
People: The day of the Powerful God is near.
Leader: This is the day of the God of darkness.
People: A great and powerful army comes in blackness. Nothing like them has ever been seen, nor will be seen in the ages to come.
Leader: Return, people, to God; come with fasting and weeping. Bring your sorrows and tears.
People: The God of Love is gracious, merciful, slow to anger, and steadfast with blessings. Despite our sins, the God of Life calls us with gentleness instead of punishment.
Leader: Blow the trumpet, call a fast, make this a holy assembly. Include the aged and the babe in arms.
People: Each one of us, in the army of blackness, is a minister unto God. Let us pray for our nation to be spared. Let us plead for our heritage, which is a mockery to many. Let us return to God until the world knows whose we are!

Invocation

Reconciling God, you invite us to be in right relationship with you. Thank you for making Jesus sin for us, so that we could become the righteousness of God. At the acceptable time we heard you call and we have accepted your day of salvation. We ask for your grace so that we will not be a stumbling block to anyone, by allowing fault to be found in our ministry. We commend ourselves unto your service. In the name of Christ we pray. Amen.

Responsive Reading Psalm 51

Leader: Self-examination and reflection on our lives cause us to plead for your love to be steady toward us.

People: It is your mercy that we need in order that our sin might be forgiven.

Leader: Hypocrisy and lies are useless in your presence. You know our inner thoughts. Cleanse us from our sin.

People: We point the finger of blame at others, but we fully participate in evil systems. Our refusal to live faithfully is sin.

Leader: We sin against you when we do not work for justice, defend the cause of the poor, provide for the homeless, or comfort our aged. The voices of neglected children and abused women are not always heard by us. It is you, Oh God, from whom we turn away.

People: If you were to turn away from us, you would be justified. If you would blot out our history and erase our name, you would be without fault.

Leader: Indeed, we are sinful and guilty, without excuse. While you require truth in all of our human efforts, we offer you deceit.

People: Wisdom of the Ages, teach us. Teach us to love ourselves, so that we might love others. Teach us to value ourselves, so that we might appreciate the worth of each one. Cleanse us from mediocrity and careless living. Wash us free of self-hate and low self-esteem. Fill us with the joy of your Holy Spirit.

Leader: Trustworthy One, erase our sins, and give us a new beginning in you.

People: Create in us a clean heart and put a new and right spirit within us. Help us see you in each other. Help us to discover and develop the creative potential you've given each of us. Let the spirit of "can do" reign within us. Restore in us the joy of freedom and sustain us as we work for liberty.

Leader: By our example, others will seek you. Because of our modeling, our youth will be inspired, our aged renewed, and our nation saved.

People: Our mouths will open wide in praise. The Lion of the Tribe of Judah is our salvation. Allowing systems to mistreat us does not please you. Playing the part of the insignificant does not bring you honor or delight But you accept our determination to talk the talk and to walk the walk of Calvary. These efforts, God, you always uphold.

Invitation to the Offering

Do not store up for yourselves treasures on earth, where thieves can take them from you. But store up for yourselves treasures in heaven. For where your treasure is, there your heart will be also.

Offertory Praise

Treasure of our hearts, we give in thanks for what you daily give to us. Allow our gifts to bless others. In your name we pray. Amen.

Benediction

Leader: Go into this season of Lent, and give!
People: We will not allow our left hand to know what our right hand is doing.
Leader: Embrace the journey to Calvary with prayer.
People: We will enter our secret closets and God will honor our prayers.
Leader: Remember the call to fast from the things that separate you from God.
People: We will recall the life of Jesus and follow in his steps. Amen.

THE FIRST SUNDAY IN LENT

Genesis 2:15–17, 3:1–7
Psalm 32
Romans 5:12–19
Matthew 4:1–11

Call to Worship

Leader: Lent is a call to collective memory.
People: We will remember God's creation, the world, the creatures, and our own genesis.
Leader: Lent is a summons to repentance.
People: We will repent of our abuse of God's creation, the world, the creatures, and ourselves.
Leader: Lent is a demand for reflection.
People: Our thoughts will focus on God's manifold gifts to us and how we may give appropriate worship and praise.

Call to Confession

In the beginning, God created. Evil came to challenge God's created beings with the question, "Has God really said?" We continue to cover our sin with this same question. Let us confess.

Confession

Creator and Creating God, you gave us such a delightful and wholesome gift in the genesis. Pride, rebellion, and lust called to us and we pulled away from you. These identical issues continue to cause sin in our lives. Rather than true confession, like the first Adam, we prefer to blame others for the troubles in our world. Forgive us our sin. Restore us to a fresh start and a new beginning. Amen.

Words of Assurance

God indeed has said, "Never will I leave you or forsake you!" This truth is our salvation. Glory to God!

Responsive Reading Psalm 32

Leader: At our very core we find contentment when our souls are right with our Creator.

People: When we are in touch with God within us, when our human relationships are built on honesty, and when we stand in solidarity with the oppressed everywhere, our spirits find great peace.

Leader: But when we stand silent and unmoved at the plight of our communities; when the victims of violence, greed, and addictions go unnoticed by us; when the prisoners of local ghettos, the lonely in nursing homes, the neglected children, and abused women go without our prayers and active support, our spirit is diminished and our humanity shrinks.

People: The hand of God is heavy upon us. Our excuses don't hold up. When we hoard even our meager contributions, we recognize our failure to participate in God's realm. When we decide to focus solely inward, our strength begins to fade.

Leader: God has reached out to us in our brokenness. When we see others with wounded spirits, damaged lives, and dashed hopes, we remember from where we have come. It is then that we acknowledge our sin and confess our faults.

People: When we allow our tears of repentance to cleanse our souls, God restores us and invites us, again, to be active in continuing the creation story.

Leader: We offer our prayers to the great Healer of spirit and soul. For we see the pain of our brothers and sisters. We want to be a part of the healing of the world.

People: We live in an age of distress, wars, bigotry, inhumanity, and indifference to the needs of "the little ones."

Leader: God is our preserver! God is our refuge! God is our deliverer!

People: The eye of God is upon us! The instruction of God is available to us. The counsel of God awaits us.

Leader: We can open doors. We can right wrongs. We can pull high places down and we can make crooked ways straight, for God is with us!

People: Anger alone will not correct evil situations. Fault finding and finger pointing will not alter the course of this world. We need God's wisdom and knowledge to lead us into corrective actions for justice.

Leader: Sin is torment and every evildoer will be punished.

People: The steadfast love of God surrounds us, despite the present situations we see with the naked eye. We rejoice in our Savior, for we are looking with the eyes of faith! And for what we see before us, we will shout for joy!

Offertory Invitation

The free gift of God is the grace made available to us in Jesus Christ. Let us share from our resources that this grace may abound throughout the world.

Offertory Praise

Bread of Life, we offer these gifts in gratitude for your providing us with a banquet in this life and beyond. Receive our gifts that the hungry of the world may be fed.

Benediction

Leader: The Living Word goes before you into the world.
People: We go with a firm determination not to yield to temptation.
Leader: Let the Word Alive dwell in you richly, motivating you to be the Word Alive in the world today.
People: We leave to worship God and to serve God's people in all that we do. Hallelujah and amen!

THE SECOND SUNDAY IN LENT

Genesis 12:1–4
Psalm 121
Romans 4:1–5, 13–17
John 3:1–17 or Matthew 17:1–9

Call to Worship

Leader: Look and live,[35] sisters and brothers!
People: Sometimes we feel like a "motherless chile,"[36] a long way from home!
Leader: Let the blind see, the lame leap, and the mute speak of God's glory everywhere.
People: Sometimes we feel like our hope is almost gone!
Leader: This is the place to be! Lift up your eyes to the hills; our help and our hope comes from the God of wonders.
People: Praise our God!

Call to Confession

Jesus heals the blind and yet we refuse to see. He heals the deaf and we continue to close our ears to the needy cries around us. The mute are made to speak and too often we remain silent in the face of injustice. Let us confess our sin.

Confession

Hope of the hopeless, you have the answer for abundant life. Yet we continue to live in a maze of uncertainty, believing we can find our own solutions. When we realize how lost we are, when our way is blocked and our answers prove absurd, we lose hope. Forgive us our sin. We want to see, we want to hear, and we want to speak in your name. Increase our faith, we pray.

Words of Assurance

The One who opens eyes, ears, and hearts has heard and already responded to our request. Love never turns us away!

Litany for International Women's Day

Leader: In the beginning, God created Eve and called her "the mother of all."

People: We remember Eve. We remember the finger of blame pointed at her, the pain it caused, and the abuse she has carried for generations. We also remember God's promise that through her salvation would come to the earth.

Leader: The story of the matriarchs includes the tale of Leah. Her father mistreated her; her husband hated her, and the strife between her and her sister was never settled.

People: We remember Leah. We remember how she has left a legacy of women having babies, trying to win the hearts of men. We also remember that God saw her plight and made her the mother of the tribe of Judah, whose praise we uplift.

Leader: The history of the Church includes Hannah, a woman abused by church and society because of her inability to bear a child.

People: We remember Hannah. The first biblical prayer of a woman is hers, as she petitioned the Throne for a son. She promised to give her child back to God; and Samuel, her son, was the first prophet and priest. We also remember the pain of all women who long for children.

Leader: Rizbah is a name seldom called. She is the foremother of Harriet Tubman, Sojourner Truth, and Rosa Parks. Her standing for the entire community is legend.

People: We remember Rizbah. We remember how she stood alone for five months, guarding not only the bodies of her two sons, but the five sons of others. She stood until God sent rain to refresh the land. The reign of justice in our world is due, in great measure, to women like her, who are bold enough to challenge injustice and stand alone.

Leader: We praise military leaders and applaud their mighty exploits. When we do the name of Deborah must be lifted.

People: We remember Deborah. We remember her hesitation in leaving her traditional and accepted roles of wife and mother to lead Israel into a winning battle. Onto the battlefield she went, her example encouraging other women to follow God into uncharted areas.

Leader: We remember the abused, neglected, and unnamed women, whose stories are important, though not often told.

People: We remember women. We remember those filled with fears and anxieties. We remember the hurt, the rejected, and the depressed. We remember those with broken dreams, crushed spirits, and aching hearts. Today, we pause to remember all women.

Leader: We remember the significant women in our lives.

People: We remember our nurturers. We remember mothers, sisters, grandmothers, sister-mothers, community-mothers, church mothers, teacher-mothers and friend-mothers. We remember their sacrifices of love, hugs, food, care, and role modeling. We remember that they had painful experiences, unrealistic expectations, and wounds of their own. They had high hopes, dreams, and visions of a day when their hearts could soar. Today, for who they were and are, we remember, with love and thanksgiving, the significant contributions of women! God bless women!

Offertory Invitation

God, who is Life-giver and Nurturer, is our provider, El Shaddai, the multibreasted one. From the more than enough, which we have already received, let's share in love.

Offertory Praise

Womb of being, in you we live, move, and have our being. We have been sustained through you. Let our gifts be used to nourish others, we pray.

Benediction

Leader: The prophet Jeremiah called for the wise and cunning women to come and lament for us.

People: Thank God for women who have cried and prayed for us.

Leader: The wisdom of God called righteous women more valuable than precious jewels.

People: Thank God for women who have modeled hope and wholeness for us.

Leader: Jesus said, "Wherever the good news is shared, it will be told in memory of her," a woman who ministered unto him.

People: Thank God for all the women whose service in God's name blesses us! Amen.

THE THIRD SUNDAY IN LENT

Exodus 17:1–7
Psalm 95
Romans 5:1–11
John 4:5–42

Call to Worship

Leader: Where will you be, when you get where you're going?
People: Why are you asking silly questions this morning?
Leader: It's the third Sunday of Lent. Are you on a serious journey to Calvary?
People: We came to enjoy church services. Why are you talking about suffering and death?
Leader: For it was the suffering and death of Jesus that gave birth to the Church.
People: Praise be to God for this priceless gift. Let's journey with Jesus to Calvary!

Call to Confession

There is a crisis in the black community everywhere. Lent says to us that there can be no sunshine theology for people who live in stormy weather! We need a clear focus and sense of direction if we are to be in solidarity with Christ. Let us confess our sin and lack of direction.

Confession

Finger of God, point us to Calvary and strengthen us to make the journey. We are lost in a wilderness of sin, where unjust laws, humiliation, and dehumanization cloak themselves as "Christian." We have stood still, grumbled, complained, and accepted lies, instead of raising the essential question of "What does God really say about my whole life?" Forgive us our sin. We quarrel with each other and depend on traditional, non-threatening, and safe worship to lead us to new life. And you send Lent!

Lent calls us to confront the status quo, to overthrow unjust systems, and to enter fully the struggle for liberation. Awaken us to the freedom you offer and, by your grace, help us embrace it with our very life. Amen.

Words of Assurance

God is among us! The Living Water desires to refresh us, revive us, and gush up in us, so that we might overflow and the whole world may drink from the fountain of life. Thanks be unto God!

Responsive Reading Psalm 25

Leader: Oh, come, let us sing to the Maker of Music. Let us make a joyful noise to the Rock of our salvation!

People: We open our mouths to give praise, but the blues more appropriately speak to our reality. We lift up our arms to offer thanks and, instead, have to fight off another closing door of opportunity!

Leader: Our God is an awesome God, filled with power and love.[37] The whole earth is in the Almighty's hands. Let us worship and bow down; let us kneel in submission.

People: Closed eyes and bowed heads have not worked to our advantage! Submission has been used by the oppressor to rob us of everything, including our dignity. A prophetic witness demands our open eyes, alert spirits, and heads lifted to confront whatever is evil and sin. The emancipator is our God, filled with relevancy for today's needs.

Leader: Oh, that today you would hear the voice of truth.

People: The ancestors listened to the "truth" as preached by oppressors, who justified our enslavement. Our foreparents reinterpreted "truth" for themselves! Truth is not blind to our suffering. Truth screams with urgency that we redeem the time. For when we fail to follow Everlasting Truth, we remain lost in the wilderness of sin.

Offertory Invitation

The Lavishly Generous Giver of Life gave us Jesus while we were yet sinners. By the saving blood of Christ we are reconciled to God. It is our privilege to extend this reconciliation by our sacrificial sharing.

Offertory Praise

Justifying God, we boast in our hope of sharing the glory of God through our giving. Because the love of God has been poured into our hearts through the Holy Spirit, we pray that these gifts spread love throughout the world.

Benediction

Leader: Go into the world and live the example of the Samaritan woman.

People: Jesus offered her living water. She responded with joy, "Give me this water!"

Leader: Go into the world and live the revelation of the Samaritan woman.

People: Jesus touched her at the point of her pain and revealed his messiahship to her first of all!

Leader: Go into the world and live the powerful witness of the Samaritan woman.

People: She convinced and converted an entire village. They came to believe in Jesus because of her liberating testimony! Amen.

THE FOURTH SUNDAY IN LENT

1 Samuel 16:1–13
Psalm 23
Ephesians 5:8–14
John 9:1–41

Call to Worship

Leader: How long will you look to political figures, powerful voices, and institutional puppets for salvation? The Searcher of Hearts is here to anoint you with power and might!

People: Can the Sacred and Intimate One use the likes of us? We don't vote as a political block, our voices are drowned in the great halls of justice, and the institutional church serves the status quo. We are too small and too insignificant to be anointed!

Leader: Always remember the older sons of Jesse. They were tall, big, strong, and powerful looking. But the God Arrayed in Mystery does not look at mere human qualities. The Guardian of our lives selects us for service by searching our hearts.

People: David was the smallest of Jesse's sons and regarded as insignificant. Mary was a virgin girl, unmarried and innocent. And the anointing Spirit poured forth on them to bring deliverance to the people of God. Today, our worship is due the God of the small and insignificant!

Call to Confession

Too often we fail to consider the strength and power of the Redeemer of the oppressed. We look at only our finite resources and become terrified at what we see. Let us confess our sin.

Confession

Helper of the Weak, to you we turn in confession and repentance. In you is found all that is good, right, and true. However, we neglect looking to you as our source. We have looked and been awed by what our naked eye can see. Forgive us our sin. Source of Blessings, restore us and anoint us with your powerful Holy Spirit, we pray.

Words of Assurance

Jesus promised, "When the Holy Spirit comes, you will have power . . . !" The promise has been fulfilled; this is our faith! Live like people with power!

Responsive Reading Psalm 23

Leader: The Quilting God is at work, on our behalf, providing us with a covering of security.

People: We can rest in comfort, blanketed by time-honored love.

Leader: From the rigid cold of hatred and the stormy blast of bigotry, we are wrapped in your warmth and revived.

People: With the scraps of life, the leftovers of equality, and the cast-offs of human dignity, the Quilting God has provided us with a sure defense of creativity and beauty, which amazes even us!

Leader: The needle, thread, and patches stitch together a sanctuary that protects and offers comfort in our most fearful circumstances.

People: The quilt is seen by the world, even by our enemies.

Leader: The intricate pattern of goodness and mercy encourages our hearts.

People: We will remain under the shelter of the Quilting God our whole life long.

Offertory Invitation

It is reasonable service to expose every unproductive work of evil. With our sharing, the good news can become visible in the world.

Offertory Praise

God of Grace and God of Glory,[38] accept our gifts in order that your goodness and mercy might bring healing to the world. Amen.

Benediction

Leader: Go into the world! Let God's glory be revealed in you.

People: We go to do the works of the Powerful One who called us here and now sends us into the world.

Leader: Go into the world! Be brilliant lights, attracting others to God's new realm

People: We go with washed eyes, able to see, and with lips ready to speak truth for ourselves.

Leader: Go into the world! Give glory to God for new vision.

People: We go, empowered by God, sent by the risen Christ, and anointed by the Holy Spirit! Hallelujah and amen!

THE FIFTH SUNDAY IN LENT

Ezekiel 37:1–14
Psalm 130
Romans 8:6–11
John 11:1–45

Call to Worship

Leader: Let's shake, rattle, and roll![39]
People: How dare you talk to us like that?
Leader: Without the refreshing Spirit of God, we are simply a valley of very dry bones.
People: Can we really be made alive? We do know that our bones are dried up, our hope is failing, and sometimes we do feel cut off from God.
Leader: The Wind of Renewal speaks, "I will put my Spirit with you, you shall live, and I will give you your own place of security."
People: The Life of the Universe has promised and will act on our behalf! We will offer praise unto our God!

Call to Confession

We are called to be God's voice and to prophesy. Yet, our words are too often irrelevant and meaningless to the issues that we face. God has spoken a powerful Word. When we fail to speak it and to live it, we have sinned. Let us confess.

Confession

Breath of Life, we have meat on our bones and breath in our bodies, but we have no power. We are a vast multitude in the world, scattered and separated. Forgive us our sin. Let the four winds come and blow upon us that we might live, fully and faithfully.

Words of Assurance

The same Spirit who raised Jesus Christ from the dead is present to give life to our mortal bodies. The Holy Spirit is available to live in us!

Responsive Reading Psalm 130

Leader: From out of a tangled web of false gods we now turn our face to the Eternal.

People: We have played the fool! We dared to trust our limited capabilities. We believed that money and education were sufficient to "belong." We looked to the political machines to make life better. All has failed. We lift our plea to your throne.

Leader: The Delight of the Ages knows us well! Despite our sins and failures, pardon is offered and forgiveness is ours.

People: Disaster lies at our doorsteps. Enemies are found within our own homes. Anxieties grip our soul and despair fills our hearts. Now, we wait on God! Our very soul waits for the faithful One. Our only assurance lies in the promises of the Guardian of our Lives.

Leader: With great watchfulness and keen scrutiny, we are alert, awaiting the arrival of the God who comes. People of color, put your hope in this God!

People: We hope in the God who will deal with our humiliation, who will heal our self-hatred, who will avenge our plight, and who will provide consolation for our aching hearts.

Leader: The God who created blackness, darkness, and the beauty of velvet midnights is the same God who is steadfast in love and has sufficient power to redeem us.

People: This God delivered Daniel. This God set Israel free. This God sent Jesus to proclaim our liberty. We will trust in this God until we die!

Offertory Invitation

To set the mind on what we can get is death. But to focus our lives on how much we can give away is life and peace in the Holy Spirit.

Offertory Praise

Spirit of Righteousness, which raised our Savior from the dead, receive our gifts and use them to spread new life in the world.

Benediction

Leader: Go, in the spirit of Mary and Martha!
People: These sisters saw approaching death and held out hope in Jesus.
Leader: Go, in the assurance of sister Martha!
People: "Yes, I believe the Messiah is the Son of God!"
Leader: Go, with the instructions of the Christ!
People: Wherever we see death, in any form, we will defy it, loose its hold, and set the bound free! Amen.

THE SIXTH SUNDAY IN LENT · PALM SUNDAY

Matthew 21:1–11
Psalm 118:1–2, 19–29

PASSION SUNDAY

Isaiah 50:4–9a
Psalm 31:9–16
Philippians 2:5–11
Matthew 26:14–27, 66

Call to Worship

Leader: Our Beginning and End has given us tongues of wisdom, that we might encourage the disconsolate with the living Word.

People: Morning after morning, our ears are made alert to new instruction from the Logos. We are taught, not by theology, philosophy, media, or even the popular opinions of our day! But our instruction comes from the Mind of the Universe!

Leader: With sound information we will not rebel, we will not back up, and we will not stop. The voice of God is in our ear.

People: We have been struck down on every side; the most hideous forms of torture have been applied to us; even today ugly remarks, nasty names, and horrible mistreatment are used towards us.

Leader: Yet the Hidden God has secured us. We have not been eradicated in total disgrace. We have learned to mask our feelings and wear our dignity, despite shameful acts.

People: The Vindicator is near! Who can stand against us in victory? We will stand together! In our unity is our strength!

Leader: Who are enemies of Christ? Let them stand and confront God face to face.

People: The Branch of Righteousness is our sure defense. We wave our palms in worship and in praise!

Call to Confession

Let the mind of Christ be in you. The mind of God emptied himself, took on our form, humbled himself, and became obedient to death on a cross for us. Therefore, let us confess our sins, which crucify him anew!

Silent Confession

Words of Assurance

Jesus is exalted to the glory of God! Every tongue that confesses that Jesus is Lord shall be saved!

Offertory Invitation

Our times are in God's hand! We have been delivered from our enemies and persecutors. Out of gratitude, let us share our resources.

Offertory Praise

Lavishly Generous God, your face shines upon us and we are saved in your steadfast love. Let our gifts reflect this love in the world.

Benediction

Leader: The parade is over! The palm branches will dry and crumble. Someone will betray Jesus!
People: Lord, is it I?
Leader: A mock trial will be held. False testimony will be given. Someone will deny Jesus!
People: Lord, is it I?
Leader: A crucifixion will take place. A sword will pierce the Savior's side. Only a few of the faithful will be found!
People: Lord, it is I!
Leader: Go in peace! Serve God's people in all you say and do! The grace of Holy Week enfold us all!

HOLY WEEK

This period of walking with Jesus to Calvary is not a usual and customary tradition in African American congregations. However, this is a prime evangelistic opportunity to reach out to your surrounding community with a soup and salad lunch followed by a short meditative worship experience. There are unchurched, previously churched, and out-of-the-area churched people who need to spend a few moments in worship as we march toward Holy Thursday, Good Friday, and Easter. The readings signal what of significance was happening to Jesus and the disciples during this last week of their ministry together.

Instead of using the Psalms as a responsive reading, I have provided a litany based upon the travels of Jesus. Following the readings, it may be helpful to provide a few moments of silence for personal reflection and meditation.

This period of walking with Jesus to Calvary is one to engage those not usually involved in the "busy life" of the congregation. Pulling together men and women who are retired to prepare the soup and salad each day gives ample opportunity for community building. Another suggestion would be to have this type of worship during each week of Lent. You may be pleasantly surprised at who will show up to a noon worship experience. Offering plates should be placed at the rear of the sanctuary and simply mentioned after the benediction. What monies are received will offset the cost of food and kitchen supplies. A particular mission in your local community can become the focus of any "additional" funds received.

Target schools, businesses, doctors' offices, and the area within a six-block radius of your building to leave flyers announcing lunch and meditation with a "free will offering." If your mission's work area is already involved with a local outreach project, mention it in your publicity. Some people who attend no congregation will be glad to give to "charity." Your church gets the credit and earns "brownie points" for caring. Invite those who "brown bag" for lunch to come and share the worship time with others as we journey to Calvary. Make this a meaningful occasion for Christ to touch hearts!

MONDAY OF HOLY WEEK

Isaiah 42:1–9
Psalm 36:5–11
Hebrews 9:11–15
John 12:1–11

Call to Worship

Leader: Here is my servant, whom I uphold, my chosen, in whom my soul delights.

People: God's spirit is upon him. Jesus will bring forth justice to the nations.

Leader: He will not cry or lift up his voice or make it heard in the street.

People: A bruised reed he will not break, and a dimly burning wick he will not quench.

Leader: Jesus will not grow faint or be crushed.

People: He is preparing to establish justice in the earth. We walk with him this week.

Call to Confession

The steadfast love of our God extends to the heavens. God's faithfulness is beyond the clouds. Our confession allows us the ability to take refuge in the shadow of God's wings. Let us pray.

Confession

The blood of goats and heifers will not satisfy the sacrifice required for us. We thank you, God, for the blood of Jesus Christ, who entered once for all into the Holy Place. Forgive us our sin. In the name of Love we pray. Amen.

Responsive Reading

Leader: Monday is the day of Jesus Christ's anointing.

People: The grateful dead was present.

Leader: Lazarus had already experienced resurrection.

People: The ungrateful thief was present.

Leader: Judas had his eye on what could be stolen.

People: Jesus was present.

Leader: And a woman anointed him as King.

People: She poured the anointing oil on his head as on a high priest.

Leader: She knelt down and worshiped at his feet.

People: The fragrance of her expensive ointment filled the room.

Leader: Instead of using the ointment for her own burial, she poured it all on Jesus.

People: The poor were present. They are yet among us. Jesus noticed them.

Leader: Her anointing prepared Jesus for the cross that was ahead.

People: A great crowd was present watching the sights, but not worshiping.

Leader: We gather to worship. We will walk with Jesus during this week of holy days.

Silence for meditation and personal reflection

Benediction:

Leader: Christ is the mediator of a new covenant.

People: We have been called to a new inheritance because of the sacrifice of Jesus.

Leader: Go in peace! Amen.

TUESDAY OF HOLY WEEK

Isaiah 49:1–7
Psalm 71
1 Corinthians 1:18–31
John 12:20–36

Call to Worship

Leader: Why have you gathered?
People: We want to see Jesus!
Leader: The Light is with us for only a little longer.
People: We will walk in the light.

Call to Confession

On this second day of Holy Week, as we walk toward Calvary, let us confess before God.

Confession

Loving God, the message of the cross is foolishness to those who are perishing, but to us who are being saved it is the power of God. Forgive us our sin. Fill us with the power to follow you.

Words of Assurance

God is never far from us. The words of our confession draw us closer to the heart of God. This is good news.

Responsive Reading

Leader: The hour is coming closer. The appointed time is near.
People: Unless a grain of wheat falls to the earth and dies, it remains just a single grain.
Leader: But if it dies, it bears much fruit.
People: Those who love their life lose it. And those who hate their life in this world will keep it for eternal life.

Leader: Whoever serves Jesus must follow. For where Jesus goes, we must go also.

People: Now my soul is troubled! And what should we say?

Leader: It was for this reason that Jesus was born to die.

People: God will get the glory.

Leader: And the world will be judged.

People: The ruler of this world will be driven out.

Leader: And Jesus will be lifted up for all the world to see.

People: We walk with Jesus to Calvary.

Silence for meditation and personal reflection

Benediction

Leader: If you walk in the darkness you do not know where you are going.

People: We leave to walk in the light. We are children of light.

Leader: The Light is with you a little longer. Go in peace!

WEDNESDAY OF HOLY WEEK

Isaiah 50:4–9
Psalm 70
Hebrews 12:1–3
John 13:21–32

Call to Worship

Leader: God has given us tongues that we might teach others.
People: God calls us to sustain the weary with our meager words.
Leader: Morning by morning God gives us alert ears.
People: God has opened our ears so we may be taught.
Leader: When we do not rebel and turn from God, we will be used in ministry to the world.
People: Let us stand up together. The Lord, our God, is our constant help.

Call to Confession

God is pleased to deliver us. We only need to ask forgiveness for our sin.

Confession

Gracious God, we have been rebellious and turned away from you. We have fallen into sin and brought disgrace to our witness. Forgive us our sin. Deliver us. Set our face like flint so that we might see no evil, hear no evil, and do no evil in your sight. Declare us "not guilty" in order that we may serve you in the world.

Words of Assurance

Therefore, since we are surrounded by so great a cloud of witnesses, let us also lay aside every weight and the sin that clings so closely, and let us run with perseverance the race that is set before us, looking to Jesus, the pioneer and perfecter of our faith, who for the sake of the joy that was set before him endured the cross, disregarding its shame, and has taken his seat at the right hand of the throne of God. Consider him who endured such hostility against himself from sinners, so that you may not grow weary or lose heart. My sisters and brothers, this is certainly good news!

Responsive Reading

Leader: The Teacher became a mother one night.
People: Jesus prepared his children a meal. He used his own body and his own blood.
Leader: The Great One became a mother one night.
People: Jesus prepared his children a bath and washed their dirty feet.
Leader: The Parent became sad one night.
People: After preparing and serving, washing and wishing, he knew betrayal was close at hand.
Leader: Jesus said, "Very truly, I tell you, one of you will betray me."
People: John asked, "Lord, who is it?"
Leader: That question continues to ring loud among us today.
People: We ask, "Lord, is it me?"

Silence for meditation and personal reflection

Benediction

Leader: We are walking with Jesus to Calvary.
People: Who among us will betray the Sovereign of Creation?
Leader: Go in peace!

HOLY THURSDAY

In the African American Church this night has been deemed appropriate for the washing of feet. It is an old custom that seems to have lost its appeal in recent generations. Yet the Savior washed the feet of his disciples on this sacred night. And we can return to this tradition, which indicates humility and service to another. If feet washing is not desired, some sort of hand washing ritual may be exchanged, with lotion provided to conclude our act of care. It is also the night that the Passover Meal is celebrated. This meal is the one eaten just before the children of Israel began their exodus from slavery in Egypt. As they were to be busy packing up and preparing for the signal to move out, the meal was to be eaten while the participants were on alert. On this night, Holy Thursday, the congregation could be asked to pack the typical meal that our ancestors might have packed as they were preparing for moving out under the cover of night for freedom. Brought in picnic baskets, this meal is a prime opportunity to celebrate together and to covenant anew to be community for each other.

Call to Worship

(Read Exodus 12:1–14.)

Song of Celebration

Call to Sharing a Meal

The feast of the slave community has always held a special place in our hearts. We can easily remember Granny packing the basket as we made ready to travel to worship, to a quilting bee, or simply to spend time with our kin. As we migrated from the south to the north and midwest, we can recall with fondness the many brown bags, packed with fried chicken, homemade rolls, deviled eggs, fried pies, and potato salad that traveled with us, in trains, buses and cars. These meals sustained us in times that the dining cars didn't welcome us. Eating together has been part of our salvation. The Jewish community has its meal, which Jesus celebrated with his friends. In that same spirit, tonight we will open our picnic baskets around the tables and share with our friends. Freedom is on the way. Let's be ready to heed its call.

Table Grace

God, you continue to call us to make haste for freedom. We thank you for your call. As we gather around these tables in celebration of the awesome ministry of Jesus to and with his friends, help us to remember his servant attitude. He prepared and served a meal. He washed the feet of his friends and affirmed them. Help us to follow his example on this holy night. Bless the abundance of food that has been prepared and that we will eat. Bless each hand that touched it in order that it grace our tables. Bless those folks with little and those with none tonight. Bless those folks who are yet willingly shackled in bondage. Sanctify this food as nourishment for our bodies. And when we leave this place, let its nutrition energize us enough to work towards the day when the world can gather around banquet tables like these with thanksgiving. In the name of Jesus Christ we pray. Amen.

After Supper Response

Congregational song of praise

Scripture Reading

(Read John 13:1–7, 31b–35)

Invitation to Servanthood

Love is an action verb. Our foreparents washed each others' feet as a sign of love, care, and service. Tonight we will offer a similar sign by washing each others' hands. Handiwipes are available at each table. After each one has cleaned another's hand, let us take the time to put lotion on that same pair of hands. Then let us pray for the ministry opportunities before our neighbors.

Hymn of Praise

Call to Communion

(1 Corinthians 11:23–26)
Communion is served.

Benediction

(Read responsively Psalm 116:1–2, 12–19)
Leader: Go in peace to love God and to serve your neighbors in all that you do.
People: Amen and amen.

GOOD FRIDAY

This worship experience is an alternative to the preaching style commonly used. This can be a worship of scripture and songs appropriate to the Word Jesus speaks. It is a time when lay speakers, young and senior, can participate in meaningful ways.

The sanctuary is dark as the congregation gathers. Acolytes enter and light altar candles. The processional of the male choir is next, followed by their acapella singing of an appropriate spiritual. When they are finished and seated the spotlight follows Jesus and Simon, slowly coming up the aisle bearing the cross. It is laid against the pulpit where it is very visible.

Call to Worship

(Isaiah 52:13–53:12)
Jesus and Simon leave as congregation stands to sing.
(Music selected by musicians)

Invocation

On this most sacred night we gather to remember. We remember the greatest sacrifice of love. We remember the journey of Jesus to the cross. We remember the price Jesus paid for our salvation. And we remember our sinfulness. We remember that his disciples ran away afraid. We remember that Jesus was left alone. Tonight, we gather to be present. Gracious God, this night, we gather to remember. Thank you for Jesus. Thank you for your presence. Thank you for your love. Thank you for this holy memory. For the sake of Jesus Christ we pray. Amen.

Scripture

(Hebrews 10:16–25)

Congregational Hymn

Seven Last Words of Jesus: The First Word
(Luke 23:26–38) *Father Forgive Them*

Solo

Seven Last Words of Jesus: The Second Word
(Luke 23:39–43) *Today You Are With Me*

Congregational Hymn

Seven Last Words of Jesus: The Third Word
(John 19:25–27) *Woman, Behold Thy Son*

Male Chorus

Seven Last Words of Jesus: The Fourth Word
(John 19:28) *I Thirst*

Congregational Hymn

Seven Last Words of Jesus: The Fifth Word
(Psalm 22) *My God, My God, Why?*

Solo

Seven Last Words of Jesus: The Sixth Word
(Luke 23:44–46) *Into Thy Hands*

The Male Chorus

Seven Last Words of Jesus: The Seventh Word
(John 19:29–30) *It Is Finished!*

The pastor invites all musical participants to the altar. Each one is given a nail for the cross. Sound effects, offstage, enlarge the sound of pounding.

The pastor invites the congregation to the altar as ushers hand out nails for taking home to remember this significant night. (Congregation can bring offering forward as they come to kneel and pray.) When the last person leaves the altar, the music ceases.

When all have finished, in silence the communion stewards strip the altar. The lights are turned off with the exception of a spotlight on the cross. There is a space of silence. The pastor instructs the congregation to leave in thanksgiving and silence. There is no additional music or talking.

HOLY SATURDAY

Call to Worship

Leader: Each of us is born.
People: Our days are too short and filled with trouble.
Leader: We come up like a flower and we wither.
People: Like a fleeting shadow we do not last.
Leader: Our days are determined.
People: Our death is certain.
Leader: Yesterday, death claimed Jesus!
People: A funeral procession followed his body to a borrowed tomb.
Leader: It is not the end of the story.
People: Thanks be to God.

Call to Confession

Mortals die. Jesus died. He was ready, prepared, and able to say, "It is finished!" Our confession helps us to stay prepared to meet death. Let us pray.

Confession:

In you, O God, we seek refuge; do not let us ever be put to shame. Forgive our sin. In your righteousness, deliver us from the bonds of death. Incline your ears to us. Rescue speedily. Be our rock of refuge and our strong fortress of salvation. Our times are in your hand. In the name of the Savior we pray.

Words of Assurance

God's face shines upon us when we confess our sin. It is with steadfast love that we are forgiven and made whole. This is good news.

Responsive Reading

Leader: A wealthy but secret disciple, Joseph of Arimathea, received the body of Jesus for burial.

People: Lord, where were your vocal followers?

Leader: Pilate allowed a secret disciple to take the wrapped body of a dead Jesus and lay it in a borrowed tomb.

People: Lord, where were your vocal followers?

Leader: A great stone was rolled in front of the door to seal the tomb. The funeral procession was very small. There were three women and one man, a disciple, at the funeral.

People: Lord, where were your vocal followers?

Leader: The chief priests and the Pharisees gathered before Pilate to plot.

People: Lord, where were your vocal followers?

Leader: They decided to put guards all around the tomb to keep Jesus locked inside a grave.

People: Lord, where were your vocal followers?

Leader: The women followers sat silent, opposite the tomb, preparing to do their last act of loving ministry to a dead corpse at the proper time.

People: Jesus died. His followers did not remember his words of assurance that he would rise. Today the whole world waits as Jesus lies in a tomb.

Leader: Lord, where are your vocal followers?

Silence for meditation and personal reflection

Benediction

Leader: If mortals die, will they live again?

People: All of the days of my life, I leave to wait until my release shall come.

Leader: Go in peace. Remember Jesus. Prepare for your death.

6 · The Easter Season

The resurrection is about our ability to rise! Jesus was tormented, mocked, caused public shame, and ultimately killed. Evil felt it had the final word. Death considered itself a victor. The grave thought itself, "the end." But Jesus got up! Evil's chain was broken. Death's hold was denied. The grave was forced to release its captive. God's power was evidenced as Jesus, the Christ, rose from the grave.

The resurrection is about our ability to be like Jesus Christ and to rise! We rise above evil circumstances. We rise above the death of hopes and dreams. We rise above our graves of depression, desolation, and despair. Every Sunday worship experience is another celebration of the resurrection. Getting up and beginning again is our theme song of joyous and unending praise.

EASTER SUNDAY

Acts 10:34–43
Psalm 118:1–2, 14–24
Colossians 3:1–4
John 20:1–18

Call to Worship

Leader: Lift up your heads, Oh, ye gates! Be ye lifted up, ye everlasting doors! The King of glory will come in. The King of glory will come in! *People:* He is risen! He is risen as he said! For the Lord has set Jesus free from the law of sin and death! This is our triumph and our call to freedom!
Leader: The Spirit of Life reigns! It reigns over violence. It reigns over gangs. It reigns over drugs and all other despair! Despite what we see in the news media, Life Abundant reigns forever!
People: All power in heaven and in earth is in the name of our risen Savior! This is our hope! This is our help! And this is our salvation! Glory and honor, celebration and praise are due the One who was and is and is to come! Alleluia and amen!

Call to Confession

Our sister Mary, who knew and loved Jesus as a brother, did not recognize him after the resurrection. We are just like her! Many are the times we go our own ways without honoring Jesus as Risen Savior and Triumphant Sovereign. Let us take this opportunity to confess our sin.

Confession

Lamb of God, who takes away the sin of the world, forgive us. Lead us not into temptation, but deliver us from evil. You are our strength and might. We have gathered with glad songs of your victory in our mouths. We repent of our sin against you and you alone. Exalt us with your powerful right hand and we shall not die, but live to recount your wonderful deeds in us. Open unto us your gates of right living that we may enter in and be saved. We will give you thanks. In the name of the Christ of glory, we pray. Amen.

Words of Assurance

We have been raised with Christ! Let us set our minds on things above, where Christ is seated at the right hand of God. For with our confession we have died and our life is hidden with Christ in God. When Christ who is our life is revealed, then we will be with him in glory. This is mighty good news! Amen!

Responsive Reading Psalm 118:1–2, 12–24

Leader: Once again we gather to give God thanks and praise for steadfast love that endures.

People: Those of the diaspora can testify with our lives that the love of God endures forever!

Leader: The spirit of death has stalked us from our African ancestors until today. It is only by God's strength and might that we can celebrate in the freedom of salvation.

Leader: We have a right to sing and to dance. The powerful hand of God continues to bring new life and new hope into our midst.

People: We shall not die! Despite the "isms" that have not died, we are yet alive! Our presence is a testimony to the wondrous survival strategies of God.

Leader: We have experienced periods of painful hopelessness. There have been days when we felt God had forgotten about us! And yet, we are alive!

People: The gates of deliverance have opened. Those who have been last are invited to enter.

Leader: Deliverance is from the Lord of Life! That life is at work in us!

People: God is our light and our salvation!

Leader: Our gifts, once so despised, have now become celebrated and sought.

People: This is God's doing, and it is a marvel in our eyes!

Leader: This is the day that God has made.

People: We will rejoice and be exceedingly glad!

Offertory Invitation

New life is a gift to be celebrated and shared. For the new life we have received in Jesus Christ, let us generously share with a waiting world.

Offertory Praise

Jesus is Sovereign, to the glory of God! The whole world needs to know it and we are the ones mandated to tell this story of amazing grace. May the love that we have shared spread the living Word. In the name of Christ, we pray. Amen.

Benediction

Leader: Go to spread the message that Christ lives and reigns forevermore!
People: We can testify that we have heard of the risen God.
Leader: Go to witness that death could not kill him and the grave did not hold him down!
People: We can verify that we have seen the risen God.
Leader: Go to tell what Jesus Christ has done in your life!
People: He lives! Christ Jesus lives today. He walks with me and talks with me, along life's narrow way. He lives! He lives! Salvation to impart. We will tell them how we know he lives! He lives within our hearts! Amen![40]

THE SECOND SUNDAY OF EASTER

Acts 2:14a, 22–32
Psalm 16
1 Peter 1:3–9
John 20:19–31

Call to Worship

Leader: What a friend we have in Jesus! All of our sins, death, and grief he bears![41]
People: What a privilege it is to come into his house, in his name, filled with power and grace.
Leader: We gather this morning to testify to the deeds of wonder and the signs of God that we have experienced in our own lives during the past week.
People: For all that we have been through, the forces of evil have not conquered our spirits nor our hopes in the resurrected Christ. Being freed from the law of sin and death, Jesus was raised from the dead. We are his body, the Church, and this conviction secures our souls. Therefore, we have assembled with glad hearts, rejoicing tongues of praise, and spirits alive with hope.
Leader: Let us worship, filled with the gladness of the presence of Christ.
People: Amen!

Call to Confession

The experiences in our lives causes us to often wonder if Christ really did win the victory over sin, death, and hell. The news media would have us believe that evil has the upper hand. The power of evil is invasive and has affected even the people of God. This is our time to confess the sin in our own lives. Let us pray.

Confession

Blessed be God, the Parent Supreme of our living Sovereign! It is by God's great mercy that the living hope of our new birth has been made possible through the resurrection of Jesus Christ from the dead. We have an inheritance that is imperishable, undefiled, and unfading, kept in the heavens for us who are protected by the power of God. Yet we have sinned and fallen short of our inheritance. God, forgive us for our sin. Grant that we may be found to be your praise and honor and glory, as Christ is revealed in our lives. In the name of Hope, we pray. Amen.

Words of Assurance

When we ask for pardon, it is in the character of God to forgive us. We can believe in the name of Christ and rejoice with an indescribable and glorious joy, for we are receiving the outcome of our faith, the salvation of our souls. Amen.

Responsive Reading Psalm 16

Leader: The siege of our communities by violence, the abandonment of our communities by viable resources, and the decaying of our communities by governmental neglect says loudly to us that our only refuge is in God.

People: The ability to pray and to call upon the strength of heaven is our greatest defense. If we abandon the God of the ancestors, we have no hope.

Leader: Regardless of where those of the diaspora are spread, their faith in God and their refusal to capitulate to the evil around them is our delight. We do remember the lessons taught at home, for they, too, entered the slave ships and remained in our collective memories.

People: There are those who have fallen captive to strange gods. They multiplied their sorrows by not having a secure anchor upon which to trust in the tests and trials of life.

Leader: Our hope is built on nothing less than the Creator of the Universe. Despite the storms of time, we have chosen to hold steady with the Captain of the Seas!

People: Downward economic trends, violence, despair, and even the current waves of attacks against us and our communities will not make us lose hope. Evil can only go so far and no farther; God sets the boundaries and we are within God's care. Our children will not be utterly destroyed; they are our heritage from the God of Love!

Leader: Wisdom is present among us. The usable stories of recovery from our past can instruct us today and tomorrow. We are the dreams of yesteryear and the visions of a new tomorrow.

People: Our history shows that we always bounce back, stronger, more encouraged, and with additional resources at our disposal. It is not the will of the enemy of our soul, but our insurance policy is the Covering God who will not drop our coverage or cancel our plan!

Leader: The hearts of the people of God can be glad. The souls of the inheritance of God can rejoice. For their well being is secured by the God of Eternity.

People: The path of life continues to stretch before us. Our journey is well mapped and even the pitfalls, delays, and obstructions come to teach us, but cannot defeat us. In this fact is joy and shalom forevermore.

Offertory Invitation

We are personal witnesses to the fact that Jesus Christ was not abandoned at Calvary and that his resurrection means new hope and new life in us. Let us share so that this Word of Truth may be spread throughout the world.

Offertory Praise

God we have a treasure contained in our earthen vessels. We want to share out of our abundance that others might come to know our great joy! Amen.

Benediction

Leader: God sends us into the world to face the fears! Go! You know you are never alone.

People: Jesus spoke, "Peace be with you" to disciples who were filled with fear.

Leader: God sends us into the world to struggle with our doubts. Go! You are not alone.

People: Jesus spoke, "Peace be with you" to disciples who were filled with doubt.

Leader: Go into the world, forgiven and filled with the Holy Spirit. In your fears and in your doubts, Christ will come and you will hear his voice saying, "Peace be with you!"

People: Jesus is Sovereign to the glory of God. Believing this, we have new life in his name. Peace is with us!

Leader: The God of the faithful, the Sovereign of peace, and the Holy Spirit bless us till we meet again! Amen and amen.

THE THIRD SUNDAY OF EASTER

Acts 2:14a, 36–41
Psalm 116:1–4, 12–19
1 Peter 1:17–23
Luke 24:13–35

Call to Worship

Leader: This is the day of interpretation.
People: Why do we need an interpreter? Are you saying that we have a foreign speaker for this morning?
Leader: Sometimes the words and ways of God are not really understood by us. With our knowledge, education, and technologies, we feel that we have it all together. But God's will for our lives continually needs to be interpreted.
People: When the Scriptures are opened up to our understanding, when we can recognize Jesus in the midst of our daily lives, and when the nonsense of our struggle is explained—in the light of God's Word, our hearts are encouraged.
Leader: Christ is risen! This morning we can interpret this message in our worship and our praise.
People: Christ is risen, indeed! Amen.

Call to Confession

Like those of long ago, we don't want to believe reports that require change in our lives. We have had to change for others so much until we feel we have given up and lost enough! Yet Christ rose that we might change, be different, even transformed. This change is not about losing, it's about gaining eternity. And that gain can begin now. Let us confess our sin, which keeps us on the losing side.

Confession

Designer of Diversity, you know that we are generous people. It is not giving that has been our problem, it's the taking we have endured. Our land and traditions have been taken. Our language and our culture have been changed, modified, and altered. Our sense of somebodiness was taken and we were made to feel bad about who you made us. We want to be in control. We want to be in charge. We want to have power. So when you come to "take" we withdraw even from you. Forgive us our sin. Take it away from us. Give us newness of life, newness of joy, and newness of hope. In the name of the One Who Gives, we pray. Amen.

Words of Assurance

When we repent we are forgiven, in the name of Jesus Christ. When our sin is taken away, we can receive the gift of the Holy Spirit. This promise is both for us and for the ones coming after us. This is the joy of our inheritance from God. Amen.

Responsive Reading Psalm 116:1–4, 12–19

Leader: Sisters and brothers, our prayers are ever before God's throne and each one of our tears is noticed. Many are the accounts in this place of God's intervention on our behalf. God is worthy of our adoration and worship. Because of an unfailing history of involvement in our lives, we know that God hears and answers prayer.

People: Death is all around us. Our children are killing each other. The pain of death is never far away in our community. We're having more funerals than weddings! It hurts to see what is happening every day.

Leader: We can call on God! We are not without resource!

People: God save us! Save our people! We pray for our own salvation.

Leader: What will you pay God for this salvation? What price can God expect from you?

People: All that we have belongs to God. We will offer ourselves as God's living sacrifice. We will continue to trust in and to call upon the name of our God.

Leader: Will you pledge allegiance to God and uplift God in your places of leisure and work?

People: We will be the faithful ones of God. Like our foreparents we will hold onto God's unchanging hand until we die.

Leader: Death does not have the final word. In Christ, God conquered death for every believer.

People: For a minute we forgot! We listened to the voice of the media. We fell for the lies of the broadcasters. We looked with only our natural eyes! But we owe God big-time thanks.

Leader: God is in the house! Give it up!

People: We give you praise, Awesome God!

Offertory Invitation

We have been bought with a high price. The auctioneers could not have asked for enough to cover our worth before God! For God did not chose silver or gold to redeem us. But God bought us with the precious blood of the Loving Lamb. In our giving we simply say, "Much obliged!"

Offertory Praise

Generous One, you have purified our souls with your obedience to the truth of God. Worthy are you to receive glory, honor, and power. With this mutual love you share with us, receive these, our gifts, so that your realm may reach the ends of the world. In thanksgiving we pray. Amen.

Benediction

Leader: Have not our hearts burned within us as the interpretation of God's love touched us anew?

People: The living and enduring Word is planted in our hearts as an imperishable seed.

Leader: Leave this place in the hope of God.

People: We leave as the Word Alive, in the world we will touch.

Leader: Leave this place in the love of Christ.

People: We leave to share this love in the places we live.

Leader: Leave this place empowered by the Holy Spirit.

People: We leave to be the Church until we meet again!

Leader: God who was and is and is to come goes before us. Amen.

People: Amen!

THE FOURTH SUNDAY OF EASTER

Acts 2:42–47
Psalm 23
I Peter 2:19–25
John 10:1–10

Call to Worship

Leader: Welcome to a service of miracles!

People: What's the information about these miracles? We just came for worship.

Leader: We are the miracles! This is our cause for worship! Think about your changed lifestyle. Think about the miracle that makes us community, family, Church.

People: You're right! We have been brought together simply because of Jesus Christ. We come from every part of this city, and from diverse walks of life. Outside of this place, many of us would never have anything in common. But we are sisters and brothers and it is a miracle. We are living signs that Christ has risen and is victorious over sin and separation. We are miracles of God's divine love. This calls for praise and worship!

Leader: This is the time and we are in the right place. Let's give it up for the Miracle Maker!

People: Alleluia! Amen!

Call to Confession

In this place it is easy to be loving, caring, and concerned. For this period of worship, each of us has goodwill towards the others who are present. Yet we go our separate ways after service and neglect the practice of community, of sharing and touching lives for God's realm. How far we have moved from both the first Church of Jesus and the customs of the ancestors. For the sin that separates us, let us pray.

Confession

Desire of the nation, what awe we experience when we remember the genuine community our foreparents had. There were no parentless children and everybody had family. Like the first Church, they were devoted to the High God and to each other. Our collective memory informs us that this is your ideal. Yet we are the beneficiaries of alienation, separation, and selfishness. We hate what we have become and desire authentic community in our life. Forgive us our sin. Restore us and we will be the Church, alive in the world. In the name of the God of all time and places, we pray. Amen.

Words of Assurance

Jesus, our friend, bore our sin in his body and we have been healed. We were going astray, but with our confession we have returned to the Guardian of our souls. This is good news.

Responsive Reading Psalm 23

Leader: The Awesome God has constructed for us a new Brewster Place community![42]

People: We are a complicated group of mixed races, diverse opinions, and differing political and economic status. Yet we're invited by God to live together.

Leader: The new Brewster Place community is a place of restoration. No bricks, cement blocks, or concrete walls will limit or impede our progress.

People: We can fully inhabit every inch of our property. For landholders have an investment that gives them security. No longer are we aliens, without land.

Leader: Our redeemed lives have been used as the earnest deposit. Jesus Christ stamped the mortgage note, "Paid in full!" The Holy Spirit provides the daily maintenance. We are only required to move in and fully engage life.

People: The former Brewster Place had great variety and community. The young and the old lived together as neighbors and friends. The poor received, for those who had, shared. This was their home.

Leader: God's Place is just like that! We are walled in and protected. We are equal in access to all that belong to a generous God. The angels act as our defense and in God's Place we are secure.

People: Goodness and mercy are in the house! They have our backs! God has provided everything we need. It sure is good to have a place we can call home! Amen.

Offertory Invitation

The Gate to New Life has issued us an invitation to live abundantly, in his house! Our sharing will extend this invitation to others around the world. Let us give in the spirit of generosity.

Offertory Praise

Amazing Grace, you have called us from death into life. You provide for our every need and call us tenderly by name. We offer our gifts so that others may have this life-giving opportunity to respond to your call. You have blessed the givers, now bless the gifts, we pray. Amen.

Benediction

Leader: Leave God's house knowing your healing is secure.
People: By the stripes of Jesus, we are healed.
Leader: Leave God's house knowing abundant life is yours.
People: By the resurrection of Jesus, we are saved.
Leader: Leave God's house knowing you are never alone.
People: Surely goodness and mercy shall follow us all the days of our lives and we shall dwell in the house of God our whole life long. Amen and amen.

THE FIFTH SUNDAY OF EASTER

Acts 7:55–60
Psalm 31:1–5, 15–16
1 Peter 2:2–10
John 14:1–14

Call to Worship

Leader: The new sounds of emerging life welcome us to this time and to this place.

People: We have only heard the sounds of sirens and boom-boxes in the night. Where did you hear these other sounds?

Leader: A distant drum is calling and the message is very clear. New life always follows death. It is the story of our Christ! Out of death came resurrection and victory for all eternity.

People: We gather this day to discern the sounds we hear and the sights we see around us. For viewing life through our natural eyes provides a dismal picture of death and destruction.

Leader: Lift up your heads. Open wide your ears. Prepare your hearts to receive what God has prepared for us.

People: Our times are in God's hand. We have come to worship and give praise. Amen.

Call to Confession

Like Thomas, we keep asking, "How can we know the way to God?" This has become our excuse for doing what we desire to do. Jesus came to show us God's love and God's way. When we follow our own wicked devices we inherit the violence and death we see around us. But there is another way. We already know it. Let us confess our sin.

Confession

Death-defying Savior, we approach you in awe and with repentance in our hearts. We know that you came to give us life and went through death and hell to ensure our salvation. Forgive us our sin. Help us to embrace the gift of pardon that you offer so freely. We are like newborn infants, and we long for your pure and spiritual milk, which causes us to grow into salvation. We have experienced rejection by others, yet we recognize how precious we are in your sight. Help us to be a holy priesthood, a spiritual sacrifice, acceptable through Jesus Christ.

Words of Assurance

Leader: Wear the kente with pride. For we are a chosen race, a royal priesthood, a holy nation, God's own people. Once we were not a people, but now we are God's people. Once we had not received mercy, but now we have received mercy from the hand of God. We can walk in the newness of life! This is good news! Amen.

Responsive Reading Psalm 31:1–5, 15–16

Leader: Forget the stocks and bonds. Don't even trust the annuities. Accumulating investment portfolios and property will not provide the security they promote. Our only hope is in God!

People: Our expectancy is of God, maker of heaven and earth. In this God we trust.

Leader: Hear our petitions for assistance. Dispatch help for our immediate situations. Rescue us from these present dangers. You have proven yourself faithful and, God, we anticipate your interventions again.

People: We are your people. We have been broken, disposed of, and rejected. Yet, we have confidence that you will guide us because we carry your name. For the sake of your honor, send liberation.

Leader: Nets, traps, and hidden plots are a way of life for us. We know that the prospect of lies, tricks, and false smiles hide behind our encounters with those who don't know our God.

People: We can fully engage life because we have the blessed assurance that a mighty God has our back!

Leader: The word in the hood is that God is yet in the house!

People: Deliverance is a large component of our history. We know the script, although sometimes we forget our part as we face our enemies and persecutors.

Leader: We are the stones that builders have rejected! We are a repeat of the Christ event. For Christ has become the very head of the corner. Our position in God is secure.

People: The Steadfast God goes before us. We will walk in the light of love.

Offertory Invitation

Stephen was the first Christian martyr, stoned for his faith. He gave his life as a prayer. Watching him die, Paul was convicted. We are not asked to give our natural life. Jesus died for us. Our financial sharing is a living prayer. Let us give that others might come to know Christ.

Offertory Praise

Our Rock and our Fortress, let these gifts be utilized to bring others to full awareness of the refuge you extend without price. We offer thanksgiving and praise with the joy of our salvation. Amen.

Benediction

Leader: Leave! Optimistic that God has a plan for you.
People: We will not allow our hearts to be troubled. We believe in God.
Leader: Leave! Confident that Christ has a place for you.
People: We know that where Jesus is, we are going. It is a prepared place, for prepared people.
Leader: Leave! Trusting in the fact that the sounds of life will lead you in the right ways.
People: We have experienced the joyful sounds that declare that Jesus is the way!
Leader: The plan of God, the place of Christ, and the peace of the Holy Spirit are ours! Amen.
People: Amen!

THE SIXTH SUNDAY OF EASTER

Acts 17:22–31
Psalm 66:8–20
1 Peter 3:13–22
John 14:15–21

Call to Worship

Leader: All around us are signs pointing to "the unknown god." Who have you come to worship this morning?

People: The God of the ancestors is the God we seek to serve. We come because our foreparents bowed before the God of eternity. This God does not change.

Leader: What are the symbols of your faith?

People: The cross symbolizes the way that our God turned death into new life. The Bible says that an ancient, oral story is alive and well today. The candles remind us that Jesus has always been the Light of the World, ever shining to lead us from slavery to freedom.

Leader: Well, come on children, let us sing praises about the goodness of the Lord![43] Amen and amen.

Call to Confession

God's existence is proven to us in our daily life. For it is in God that we live and move and have our being. We have no need to grope and to search for God. It is we who leave. God never withdraws from us. Let us confess our sin, which separates us.

Confession

God, you command that people everywhere repent, for you have established a day when you will judge the world in righteousness. We ask your forgiveness for our sin. We want to do you proud as your offspring. And we have failed. We stand in need of your amazing grace, which washes and makes us clean before you. In the name of Jesus Christ, we pray. Amen.

Words of Assurance

The God of all beings has provided a fuller's soap for our cleanliness. The blood of Christ has been poured forth to wash away our sin. It is the good pleasure of God to restore us to right relationship and to grant us shalom. Amen.

Responsive Reading Psalm 66:8–20

Leader: Ancient of Days, we are struggling to speak your praise. The sounds of grief, pain, and anguish are so loud in our ears.

People: Children killing children has become a way of life in our communities. It seems as if we are slipping into retrenchment from our communities' morals, values, and ethics.

Leader: You have permitted us some difficult days in our past. We have been stretched and tested to the limits of human endurance.

People: We have been made the burden bearers for others.

Leader: They thought we were inferior, simply because we could work so hard. We have suffered untold misery because of being strong of will and body. We endured and we survived. God has brought us to a new position in life.

People: We will not go backwards! We will give God, who is with us, praise. We will remember where God brought us from and be encouraged.

Leader: When trouble comes, when danger is sensed, we get afraid. Fear causes us to forget that the Ultimate One is in charge.

People: We need only rehearse our story. The deeds and exploits of God are contained in it. The turning of events for our benefit, the interventions on our behalf, and the interference of God in plots and plans against us are legends worth hearing again.

Leader: Tell the story. Let's listen with our hearts. The message has not changed. Jesus saves!

People: From the projects to the statehouse, from the prison cell to the Capitol floor, from the hospice to the birthing room, Jesus saves! Our salvation is in him.

Leader: God hears our cries. Falling souls are caught by the reach of God. Feeble cries are heard by the ears of God. Have a little talk with Jesus. It's going to be all right.[44] Amen.

Offertory Invitation

Sanctify the Lord in your hearts! From hearts filled with gratitude for the resurrection of Christ, who now sits at the right hand of God, interceding for us, let us share.

Offertory Praise

Christ, you suffered for our sins to bring us to God. Accept this our humble thanks and use it to win others to new life in you. Amen.

Benediction

Leader: Love God and keep the commandments as you live and work this week.
People: The Advocate, the Holy Spirit, goes with us into the world.
Leader: You are never alone.
People: Jesus is Sovereign to the glory of God. Believing this, we have new life in his name. Peace is with us!
Leader: The God of the faithful, the Son of shalom, and the Holy Spirit bless us until we meet again. Amen and amen.

ASCENSION SUNDAY · SEVENTH SUNDAY AFTER EASTER

Acts 1:1–11
Psalm 47
Ephesians 1:15–23
Luke 24:44–53

Call to Worship

Leader: The world doesn't like it. Too often we don't understand it. But we have been chosen!

People: Of course we have been chosen. We have been chosen to be the "mules of the earth,"[45] despised because of the color of our skin.

Leader: That's only part of our story! And how we can continue to hold on, look up, and remain the faithful people of God—that's what the world doesn't quite comprehend.

People: We do it because of the living presence of the Holy Spirit, who was promised by Jesus Christ on the day he was lifted on a cloud and received back into the heavens with power.

Leader: Jesus died and rose again for our salvation. His ascension released the power of God to dwell in us and work through us despite the realities we face in life.

People: And for this reason we sing in times of trouble. We can stand in the face of opposition. And we can trust God, who is faithful and keeps every promise.

Leader: Why are we standing here? There really is no debate. We have been chosen to offer our praise.

People: We lift our hearts in grateful praise. Amen.

Call to Confession

Jesus Christ came to open our understanding and to give us a spirit of wisdom and knowledge, so that with enlightened hearts we might realize this glorious opportunity we have to be in personal relationship with God. This is our inheritance, which is immeasurably great and awesome in its power. Let us confess our sin, which keeps us from living out of these riches. Let us pray.

Confession

Awesome God, the fullness of your glory frightens us. We try to come close, we want to be in relationship with you, but we are afraid. We see how you allowed Jesus to be rejected, to suffer, and to die. We seek to find a different route to you. Forgive us our sin. Work your holy power in us and help us to live fully in your grace. Creative Source of Ascendancy, lift us now, we pray. Amen.

Words of Assurance

You will receive power when the Holy Spirit comes upon you; and you will witness for God in all the world. God has already put this power to work in Christ who is now seated in the heavenly places far above all rule and authority and power and dominion, with a name above every name. This Jesus is head of the church, which is his body. Thank God we are included. Amen.

Responsive Reading Psalm 47

Leader: It's time to participate in the worship and to offer up songs of joy to our God.
People: Our God is an awesome God.[46]
Leader: The Ruler of the Universe has the whole world in hand.
People: Our God is an awesome God.
Leader: Our heritage has been preserved; our lives have been redeemed by grace.
People: Our God is an awesome God.
Leader: Deliverance has come, even to South Africa, which was captive to apartheid and death.
People: Our God is an awesome God.
Leader: With a shout heard around the world, Nelson Mandela was released from prison.
People: Our God is an awesome God.
Leader: The shuffling of feet has picked up the beat to become the dance of victory and praise.
People: Our God is an awesome God.
Leader: "We shall overcome!"[47] is the former victims' song and battle cry.

People: Our God is an awesome God.
Leader: God is enthroned in glory! The royalty of God walks the face of the earth.
People: Our God is an awesome God.
Leader: The Highly Exalted Shield of the Earth is our protector and our God.
People: Our God is an awesome God.

Offertory Invitation

God had faith enough in us to leave the continuation of the church in our hands. For this reason we must share generously. With our sharing the proclamation of the story goes on.

Offertory Praise

Ascended One, as you have raised us to sit in heavenly places with you, receive our gifts so that others might be lifted and come to know you in the power of your resurrection. Amen.

Benediction

Leader: God bless you!
People: God has endowed us with power.
Leader: God consecrate your work, your leisure, and your life.
People: God has anointed us to be representatives of the new realm.
Leader: God grant you joy in service.
People: God has put a song in our hearts to lift us up where we belong.
Leader: God keep you in victorious power, as the wind beneath your wings. Until we meet again!
People: Amen and amen!

THE SEVENTH SUNDAY OF EASTER

Acts 1:6–14
Psalm 68:1–10, 32–35
1 Peter 4:12–14, 5:6–11
John 17:1–11

Call to Worship

Leader: It's Hammer time![48]

People: Have you lost your mind? This is Sunday morning worship, not "Hammer time!"

Leader: Listen up! God took a victim's death and smashed it all to pieces, rearranged it and made the victim and the cross symbols of victory and triumph.

People: Interesting thought, but there is violence and danger all around us. We don't see much victory and triumph.

Leader: Beloved, do not be surprised at the fiery ordeal that is taking place around us, testing us, as though something strange is happening to us. Always remember! God took the Creative Power of the Universe, reversed it, and had it live the painful life of a rejected human. Then God took that life, crushed it, and raised it up as the firstborn of the Church.

People: You sure can't touch that! It might not be Hammer time, but it sure is time to give praise and honor to the God of Eternity who continues to allow us to rejoice even as we share Christ's sufferings. We have gathered to be glad and to shout for joy, because we are blessed with the Spirit of God in the midst of our situations. This God is worthy of our praise. Amen.

Call to Confession

Jesus Christ has come and gone. And we continue to stargaze, to wander and seek for other saviors. The angels asked the first disciples what they were looking for. The question is yet appropriate for disciples today. This same Jesus is coming again soon. Let us confess our sin and be ready for his return.

Confession

God of Awe and Wonder, we really do look foolish at times. We sit and reflect. We walk and we talk. We ponder and pontificate as if we don't know what we have been assigned and required to accomplish for you. Jesus gave us the example and showed us how to live. Forgive us our sin. Help us to cast our cares and concerns on you, for we know that you care for us. In the name of the Lamb of the World, we pray. Amen.

Words of Assurance

When we humble ourselves before God, with honest confession, it is the grace of God that will restore, support, strengthen, and establish us in eternal glory. This is the Word of God for the people of God. Amen.

Responsive Reading Psalm 68:1–10, 32–35

Leader: God is on the move! Those who show disrespect will be brought down. All of those who serve other gods will be kicked to the curbs in short order.

People: Come, we who love the Lord, and let our joys be known!

Leader: There is a song in our hearts. There are untold melodies on our lips. For our God is worthy of songs of praise and delight.

People: The neglected and the orphan have a new song to sing, for God has a rep with the little and the forgotten ones of the world.

Leader: The homeless and the wayward have a shelter. The captives to addictions and compulsions have a way up and out. But those who refuse God's hand of help are doomed.

People: Before the beginning, God was at work, making provisions for us, taking the desolate and void, making a place of wonder and delight for our habitation.

Leader: The rich, black soil was dense and the mountain ranges high as God spoke the motherland into existence. The God of Africa, the High God, reigned in splendor.

People: We were an abundant people. Then the diaspora took us abroad. Yet God has maintained our heritage, even when it seemed to languish.

Leader: In strange lands we have been made to dwell. In different climates we have learned to adjust. In different cultures we have remained distinct. God's goodness provided for our needs.

People: From around the world, we of the diaspora continue to lift our characteristic sounds of praise in exultation of our God.

Leader: The ancient listen. In concord, for this divine providence, their voices join in acclamation.

People: Regal Power and Sovereign Majesty is the name of our God.

Leader: God is in the house!

People: Our God is an awesome God! Blessed be God!

Offertory Invitation

The authority of Jesus Christ belongs to us! He won eternal life for all of us who call upon his name. It is our high privilege to share our resources in order that others might come to know him.

Offertory Praise

The work of Jesus Christ was finished at Calvary. The task is now left in our hands. Please receive our gifts of labor that the ministry may continue until the world comes to know him as Savior and Sovereign. Amen.

Benediction

Leader: God sends you into the world. Go! Keep alert, for the adversary of our souls is looking for someone to devour.

People: We go, steadfast in our faith, for we know God. And we know that our brothers and sisters in all the world are undergoing the same kinds of suffering and tests.

Leader: God sends you into the world. Go! Because the spirit of glory, which is the Spirit of God, is resting upon us.

People: We go, in the power of the Word and the name.

Leader: The strong name of God, the salvation of Jesus Christ, and the power of the Holy Spirit go before us. Amen.

6 · Pentecost and the Following Season

The Holy Spirit arrives fresh, hot, touching, laughing, anointing, and dispatching the hidden and scared individuals into the streets. The Holy Spirit, the comforter, sent to live in us, work on us, walk beside us to guide our daily life, comes on the scene. It's a time for celebration. It's a distinct and significant occasion, for power is in the house! It's a brand new day, a brand new beginning, and a brand new season of growth, spread, and change.

"You will receive power" is the promise of Acts 1:8. The Holy Spirit's power is necessary for the effective living of our new life in Christ. The acts and deeds of those called Christian will be noticed by all the world. The power to make a difference is ours!

Ordinary time—the long period between Pentecost and Advent—is the longest season of the Church, where we are called to live out our faith on a daily basis without any festival to celebrate. As we walk with God on a daily basis, in the mundane duties of regular existence, the worship rituals, our daily devotions, and our life of prayer will see us through.

Altar Focus

For Pentecost, red with white paraments and red balloons are needed to set the stage for fire, which not only burns and consumes, but ignites, motivates, and inspires. Red candles of assorted sizes and shapes would make a lovely addition. A banner with tongues of fire laid across the altar can assist in delivering the message of a brand new day.

The liturgical color for ordinary time is green to signify growth, which God continues to anticipate from our lives as we live without fanfare and hoopla.

PENTECOST SUNDAY

Numbers 11:24–30
Psalm 104:24–34, 35b
Acts 2:1–21
John 20:19–23

Call to Worship

Leader: This is the morning of commencement and the day of new beginnings![49]
People: We have come from diverse parts of town. We have gathered with divergent backgrounds and positions. We even have different needs and expectations.
Leader: We are just like the first Church! Scared, confused, some were unemployed. But they came together, and as they waited and prayed the Holy Spirit came afresh and anew.
People: There were tongues of fire and the noise of wind. The room was shaken and they were changed. Amazed and astonished, they left that room and changed the world for God.
Leader: This is our day. This is our time. The Holy Spirit awaits us. This is the morning of commencement.
People: This is the day of new beginnings. Praise God! Amen.

Call to Confession

With sound, sight, and speech, the disciples were made aware of a powerful addition to their lives. They went out into the city and begin to witness to the wonderful deeds of Jesus Christ in their lives. That same power belongs to the Church today. Let us confess our sin, which renders us powerless and ineffective in our witness.

Confession

God of powerful signs, we pause to offer our worship. But sin blocks our relationship. Forgive us our sin. Pour out your Holy Spirit upon us, so that your sons and daughters prophesy, your young men see visions, and your old men dream dreams. We call upon your name and want to be saved. In the power of Christ, we pray. Amen.

Words of Assurance

Everyone who calls upon the name of the Lord, shall be saved. For in the one Spirit we were all baptized into one body and we were all made to drink of one Spirit. This is good news. Amen.

Responsive Reading Psalm 104:24–34, 35b

Leader: The works of God are many and great!
People: The wisdom of God is vast and deep!
Leader: The expanse of God's creation is immense and majestic!
People: All things must bow before God, every living thing, both small and large.
Leader: Whether enormous in stature or insignificant of being, they were formed by God.
People: And when the deal is done, money nor position will matter, for the breathe in every body comes from the grace of God.

Invitation to Offering

Jesus is Sovereign to the glory of God! And now there are varieties of gifts, but the same Spirit; and there are varieties of services, but the same God who activates all of them in everyone. To each is given the evidence of the Holy Spirit for the common good. To continue the promotion of the work of the Holy Spirit in the world, let us share our resources.

Offertory Praise

Spirit of Life, we celebrate you. Thank you for blowing afresh upon our spirits, renewing us and granting us the high pleasure of sharing what we have. Grant that these gifts may be used to spread the joy of Jesus in our world. Amen.

Benediction and Blessing

Leader: Peace be with you!
People: Peace be with you!
Leader: Receive the gift of the Holy Spirit and be signs and wonders in the world you will touch. Leave called by God, claimed by Christ, and baptized by the Holy Spirit. Make new disciples everywhere you go! Amen.
People: Amen.

TRINITY SUNDAY · FIRST SUNDAY AFTER PENTECOST

Genesis 1:1–2:4
Psalm 8
2 Corinthians 13:1–13
Matthew 28:16–20

Call to Worship

Leader: In a world filled with news of the demise of household values, we gather today, because it is a family affair!
People: We offer praise to the Trinity: Creator, Son, and Holy Spirit.
Leader: The Maker, Redeemer, and Sustainer of all have joined in corporate unity to form a new creation story.
People: The new creation is in us. The new creation is for us. The new creation is us!
Leader: In the midst of our gloom and despair, in the voids of our loneliness and searching, the family of God speaks newness, growth, and fruitfulness into our existence and we come to know that "it is good."
People: Speak to us again, recreate us and we will be a household of faith. We worship the triune God.

Call to Confession

We are made in the image of God! Our intelligence, our soulfulness, and our very being are filled with the creative design of the Pure Divine! Yet we forget. We have listened to those voices that have declared that "you are not good!" We have bought into the lie of evil. And we have left the heritage of kindred relationships established for us "in the beginning!" Let us confess our sin.

Confession

Triad of Holiness, the gifts you bequeathed to us are many and great. How excellently you made us, how exceptional was your strategy for us, how generous was your dream of what we would accomplish as your family on the earth. What a mess we have made. Forgive us our sin. Restore us to a vivid concept of our possibilities. Revive our sense of familial relations. And reestablish in us the unity found in you. In the name of Blessed Oneness, we pray. Amen.

Words of Assurance

"In the beginning" signifies the hope, optimism, and desire that starts afresh, whenever we confess our sin and return to God. "In the beginning" means the new start God provides for the recreative process in the chaos of our lives. "In the beginning" God will speak words of assurance to our souls. Thank God for this present moment, which is our personal rendezvous with "the beginning." Amen.

Responsive Reading Psalm 8

Leader: Sovereign God, the strength of your name has infused the complete world.

People: On the heights of the heavens, in the depths of the seas, from the east to the west, and from the south to the north the potency of your name is established.

Leader: The winding Tigris and Euphrates Rivers and the vast sweep of African plains are engraved with the exalted name of the High God.

People: The mouths of our ancients spoke of your praise.

Leader: Ptah-Hotep, 2,500 years before the birth of Christ; Akhenaton, 1,385 years before your appearance on the earth; and Aesop, 620 years before you made yourself visible to our eyes, each sang of your glory in poetic tribute.

People: In the infancy of human formation, the Preeminent One was extolled.

Leader: Your prints were engraved in nature, your beauty was enshrined in each human's eyes, and your love was woven into the texture of the land.

People: What are we, made of rich, black soil, that you would care for us?

Leader: Yet you created us a little lower than the angels. You crowned us with the honor of your brilliant mind and the power of creation. You gave us dominance over the things you fashioned for our enjoyment and made them subject unto us.

People: What authority you gave us! What a capacity for notable deeds and exploits is ours!

Leader: Sovereign God, how majestic is your name and attributes in us!

Call to the Offering

With the authority of "in the beginning" also comes the responsibility of continuation. To ensure the proper spread of the work of new creation, we share our resources with grateful hearts. The Lavishly Generous God loves a cheerful giver.

Offertory Praise

Giver of New Beginnings, receive our praise and thanks. Let the spread of your realm take the wings of the morning and fly to searching hearts needing restoration and recreation, we pray. Amen.

Benediction

Leader: Finally, brothers and sisters, farewell. Put things in order, listen to my appeal, agree with one another, and live in peace.
People: The God of love and peace will be with us.
Leader: Greet one another with a holy kiss.
People: All the saints greet you.
Leader: The grace of our Sovereign, Jesus Christ, the love of God, and the communion of the Holy Spirit be with us all. Amen.

PROPER 4 · SUNDAY BETWEEN MAY 29 AND JUNE 4

Genesis 6:6–22, 7:4, 8:1–19
Psalm 46
Romans 1:16–17, 3:22–31
Matthew 7:21–29

Call to Worship

Leader: The storms rage, the winds of distress blow, and the rains of terror often beat upon us, but we have come to the Ark of Safety.
People: Salvation is of God.
Leader: We have a sure haven, designed by God, to protect us from the destruction going on around us.
People: Salvation is of God.
Leader: God established a covenant with Noah and with us, to keep him and his family safe from the horrors and alarms. The Designer of Sanctuary locked the doors against destruction, put one window in the top of the ark and instructed us to "Look Up!"
People: Salvation is of God. The covenant is secure. And, we offer praise unto our God.

Call to Confession

All of us have sinned and fallen short of the glory of God. Justification is offered to us now, as a gift of grace, through the redemption that is in Jesus Christ. Let us confess our sin.

Confession

God, we work harder and harder to prove that we are righteous. We strive to show evidence of our faith by the things we do and accomplish. Yet we know that salvation is ours through faith. Forgive us our sin. Destroy the yokes of righteousness by works, which pull us away from you and from each other. Restore us to right relationship with you. In the name of our Redeemer and Sanctifier, we pray. Amen.

Words of Assurance

I am not ashamed of the gospel; it is the power of God for salvation to everyone who has faith, to the Jew first and also to the Greek. For in it the righteousness of God is revealed through faith for faith; as it is written, "The one who is righteous will live by faith." Our faith makes us whole. This is the Word of God for the people of God! Amen.

Responsive Reading Psalm 46

Leader: Our God is a haven and a fortress. It is reassuring to know that we always have a strong tower and protection that time nor trouble can move nor diminish.

People: We have lived with the signs of violence and destruction around us. Our world has not been one of quietude and solace. But we have had to endure making a life in the midst of difficulties and transitions.

Leader: Our legs have felt like water and our heads have been aswirl with confusion over "tomorrow." Oft times our very foundations have been shaken by the realities we must face.

People: Then we turn to the Ancient of Days, whose security and permanence is the only place of stability we know.

Leader: God is always in the house! This is the fact upon which we base our life. God will hear our faintest cry and restore our faltering steps.

People: The world around us is always shaky and unstable. World leaders topple like the toys of children. What was is no longer and what will be we cannot conceive.

Leader: But our confidence is in the eternal God who remains steadfast and unmovable.

People: The violence and horror we see today is no worse than we have had used against us before. Our history reminds us that temporary alarms don't have the last word.

Leader: Just think of God's goodness and remember how far we have come. In the midst of terror, "Be still and know God!"

People: The High God of the ancestors is with us; the God of the ancients is our retreat.

Offertory Invitation

"Not everyone who says, 'Lord, Lord,' will enter the kingdom of heaven," only those who know the will of God. As we share, we do so in the confidence that others will hear and then build their house on our Rock! Our giving enlarges the new realm.

Offertory Praise

God, your righteousness is revealed in our sharing. You have given us and we return it to you, out of the sincerity of our hearts. May the money that we share spread this gospel throughout the world. Amen.

Benediction

Leader: The rains will continue to fall, the floods will keep coming, and the winds will come to beat upon your house. But, go in the name of Jesus.
People: We have staked our security in the One who has never failed. We leave in the strength of God.
Leader: You have heard the Word of life, may it become life in you for the journey ahead.
People: We will act upon what we have learned and walk in the path of righteousness.
Leader: The love of God, the grace of Christ, and the authority of the Holy Spirit make you bold and faithful witnesses in the world this week. Amen.

PROPER 5 · SUNDAY BETWEEN JUNE 5 AND JUNE 11

Genesis 12:1–9
Psalm 33:1–12
Romans 4:13–25
Matthew 9:9–13, 18–26

Call to Worship

Leader: The realm of God is always about moving, packing up, leaving the familiar, and going into the distant unknown.
People: The promise of God is for a great nation, untold blessings, and a great name.
Leader: The transitions, shifts, and passages of our lives are the necessary prerequisites to receiving the promises of God.
People: The promise of God is for a great nation, untold blessings, and a great name.
Leader: We would like to know security, permanence, and a settled existence, but we are always called to journey.
People: The promise of God is for a great nation, untold blessings, and a great name.
Leader: The preservation of our nation, the blessings of posterity, and a name established in the earth is our heritage from God.
People: To the Promise Keeper we give praise. Amen.

Call to Confession

The promise that he would inherit the world did not come to Abraham or to his descendants through the law but through the righteousness of faith. Without active faith it is impossible for us to please God and inherit the promises. Let us confess the sin that blocks our faith.

Confession

God of promise and faithfulness, we have traveled great distances, given up all that was "home," been sojourners in a strange land, and yet held onto faith in you. We have waited, watched, and hoped. We have been disappointed, depressed, and filled with despair as others have seemed to inherit everything and left us among the dispossessed. In our search for our own fulfillment, we have sinned. Forgive us our sin, we pray. In the name of the promised Son, amen.

Words of Assurance

Like us, Abraham hoped against hope, tried to help God make the promise come sooner, and found himself in a mess. But also like us, he did not weaken in the faith. Distrust did not make him doubt God's ability to perform the promise. It was his faith, and ours, that God counts as righteousness. This is good news! Amen.

Responsive Reading Psalm 33:1–12

Leader: Let the faithful to God rejoice and be glad. For the joy of the Sovereign God is our strength.

People: The benefits of praise have served us well! With our music, our feet, and our words we lift high the name of our God.

Leader: Our gospel music is an articulation of celebration. Our jazz music is soulful eloquence with a slower beat. Our blues is the gut-wrenching cry of hurting hearts and broken spirits when hope is almost gone. The meter is not important; singing before God is our intent.

People: The Ancient of Days is faithful and worthy to be praised.

Leader: The highest praise we can offer before God are lives of justice and right living.

People: The Word of God created the world and breathed life into our foreparents.

Leader: Chaos was given limits and turbulent waters were harnessed and tamed.

People: Our God is an awesome God![50] Let all the world stand in reverent honor of the Divine Designer.

Leader: God's Word commands, creates, and maintains the universe.

People: The leaders of the world are as powerless as the toys of children before the Creator. All of their grand plans and schemes are frustrated by God's will.

Leader: The mind of God stands forever. The promises of God are firm and sure. The thoughts God had for the prosperity, abundance, and affluence of the ancestors live on for us. Time and situations have not altered the heart of God.

People: We are the heritage of God, chosen and preserved through our generations. Happy is the nation whose sovereign is God.

Offertory Invitation

Jesus Christ continues to call "follow me!" This call is to sacrificial living and sharing. Let us follow Jesus in our giving.

Offertory Praise

Gracious Savior, you declared that you came to call sinners to your realm. You have called us and we have answered with joy. Receive our gifts and use them so that the work of calling might continue to reap a harvest of souls. Amen.

Benediction

Leader: We are sent into the world to touch lives, heal disease, and resurrect the dead.

People: We will follow the example of our Savior, who called us and goes before us.

Leader: The world will mock you, laugh at you, and think you are foolish.

People: We will follow the example of our Redeemer, who called us and goes before us.

Leader: The sick, the suffering, and the oppressed await your arrival this week.

People: We will go in the power of the Holy Spirit who dwells in us and empowers us.

Leader: The creative energy of God, the healing compassion of Christ, and the dynamism of the Holy Spirit are ours. Amen.

PROPER 6 · SUNDAY BETWEEN JUNE 12 AND JUNE 18

Genesis 18:1–15, 21:1–7
Psalm 116:1–2, 12–19
Romans 5:1–8
Matthew 9:35–10:8 (9–23)

Call to Worship

Leader: The Christ will encounter us at the most unexpected times and in the least likely places.
People: We are on the alert for signs of God.
Leader: Hospitality demands that we be prepared, with open hearts and minds.
People: We have come ready to greet and engage the Almighty.
Leader: What do you bring as evidence of your readiness for God?
People: Songs of Zion are in our hearts, words of praise are in our mouth, and our spirits are willing to receive fresh manna from on high.
Leader: The stage is set for worship!
People: Amen!

Call to Confession

In our hustle and bustle of living we often forget to look for Christ. Yet Christ is among us waiting to be discovered. Our oversight is spiritual blindness. Our neglect of seeing each other and the needs is sin. Let us confess our sin and receive our sight.

Confession

All-Seeing Sovereign, we approach you to ask forgiveness of our sin. We have allowed the cares of our personal lives to close our eyes to the world around us. We have not opened our eyes to the needy among us. We have felt hemmed in by the many needs of our own lives. So we didn't look to see who else mattered to you. Wash us and make us clean. Open our eyes and help us to see you in others. Lift our hands to be willing workers in your service. In the name of the One Who Cares, we pray. Amen.

Words of Assurance

When Abraham and Sarah laughed at the promises given in their old age, God yet came. Their skepticism did not defer God's plan. The question asked them, "Is anything too hard for God?" was answered with the joy of new life. This is our assurance and it is good news. Amen.

Responsive Reading Psalm 116:1–2, 12–19

Leader: Even before Goree Island and the journey of no return from our home, God was there, weeping with us, listening to our groans and moans, heeding our petitions for deliverance.

People: In tightly packed ship hulls, the human cargo's excruciating cries were heard and answered; the seas trembled under the weight of our agony, and the wind exhaled in pain.

Leader: The universe lent its sorrow to our plight and God's care was provided. The ear of God is always open to our cries.

People: We are the survivors of the most fit! The slave trade was a business of international proportion. Its ugliness spread its tentacles to every port along the way. Like chattel, worse than animals, our foreparents were bargained for, bought, and sold. But it's because of God's mercies that we were not made extinct!

Leader: What can we pay God for this, our debt of life and posterity?

People: We can be faithful, steadfast, and committed to the God of the ancestors.

Leader: Our life can be a testimony about the goodness of our God.

People: Precious in the eyes of God are all of those who have died in the faith.

Leader: Our experiences in this strange land have not made us forget the High God. Like our foreparents, we belong to the Almighty.

People: To give thanks for a journey such as we have had often demands a sacrifice of our praise.

Leader: Yet despite a painful past, we continue to reverence, honor, and worship God.

People: God's house is a safe place. God's house is a refuge. God's house is our home. Here we are renewed, refreshed, and restored. We bless the name of God.

Offertory Invitation

Therefore, since we are justified by faith, we have peace with God through our Lord Jesus Christ, through whom we have obtained access to this grace in which we stand. What a gift we have received. Let us share from the gratitude of our spirits.

Offertory Praise

Lavishly Generous God, your love has been poured into our hearts through the gift of the Holy Spirit. For while we were sinners, Christ died for us. Receive our gifts of love so that others might come to know and experience you. In the name of Love, we pray. Amen.

Benediction

Leader: Jesus went about, teaching, proclaiming the good news, and curing disease and sickness. Leave to do the same.

People: The harvest is plentiful, but the laborers are few. We go with the authority to be disciples of Jesus Christ.

Leader: As you go, proclaim that the realm of Christ has come.

People: We have received without price; we leave to give what we have received without charge.

Leader: The love of God, the authority of Christ, and the healing power of the Holy Spirit go before us. Amen.

PROPER 7 · JUNETEENTH OBSERVANCE

SUNDAY BETWEEN JUNE 19 AND JUNE 25

Genesis 21:8–21
Psalm 86:1–10, 16–17
Romans 6:1b–11
Matthew 10:24–39

Call to Worship

Leader: Welcome to Celebration Station! We have gathered to shout for the joy of freedom.
People: How did you feel when you come out the wilderness?[51]
Leader: Hagar, the Egyptian woman, was forced into the desert with her son, but there God promised them freedom!
People: How did you feel when you come out the wilderness?
Leader: For over two hundred years, we were forced to survive in the "wilderness" of slavery. But on June 19, 1865, the southern slaves found out they were free and celebrated the first Juneteenth.
People: How did you feel when you come out the wilderness?
Leader: Jesus, our Christ, spent his time in the wilderness and walked out with our freedom in his mind.
People: We have come to celebrate the wilderness. For we are leaning on the Lord!

Call to Confession

Like Hagar, it is often that we are forced into unfriendly situations through no fault of our own. In the wilderness of our lives, we get afraid and get down on God. Let us take this opportunity to confess our sin, which keeps us stuck in the wilderness instead of allowing us to pass through to new horizons.

Confession

God of the wilderness, forgive us our sin. We have become accustomed to being in the wilderness, fighting for our survival and feeling that we have to make it on our own. Help us to hear your voice and to know that your presence is near to guide us through every desert experience. In your name, we pray. Amen.

Words of Assurance

The angel of God called to Hagar when she felt most bereft and alone. She was told not to be afraid, for God had heard her cry. Then she received the same promise of Abraham, that her son would become a great nation! Our times in the wilderness always reap tremendous benefits when we wait and hear God. This is good news! Amen.

Responsive Reading Psalm 86:1–10, 16–17

Leader: God heard the cries arise from the deltas of this land.

People: The stooped backs and heavy sacks, dragging the cotton and tobacco fields, did not prevent the whisper of prayers, which reached the ears of God.

Leader: Come by here, good Lord, come by here![52]

People: Way down here, all by myself, and I can't hear nobody pray!

Leader: But I trust in God, wherever I may be!

People: God, you is a mighty good God and you don't ever change![53]

Leader: Emancipation came!

People: But another crop had to be made and the news of freedom was slow in working its way south to the ears of those who never gave up hope and refused to give up praying.

Leader: Emancipation came!

People: The sweet taste of freedom arrived late, but arrived, nevertheless. God heard our cries.

Leader: God is a great God who does great and mighty things for us, whereof we are glad!

People: God seldom comes when we want, but whenever God shows up, it's right on time!

Leader: Some celebrate independence from England. We celebrate the day that God delivered us from the wilderness of slavery in this land! Juneteenth is a sign of God's favor towards us and a symbol of comfort to our souls.

People: The end of slavery is a gradual process and the journey out of the wilderness continues with God's help.

Offertory Invitation

We have been raised from death to life! By the unmerited favor of new life in Christ, we have been freed from sin. Let us give in order that others might know this privilege and joy.

Offertory Praise

Giver of Life, you died to sin, in order that we might live again. Accept our offerings of love, given so that others might come to know you and live with you throughout eternity.

Benediction

Leader: A disciple is not above the teacher! And Jesus spent time wrestling in the wilderness.

People: We leave, not afraid of the wilderness, but sustained by the voice of God.

Leader: You have been saved and delivered from many desert places. Remember Juneteenth!

People: God is working, even when we have not received the news! We will be faithful in difficult times.

Leader: Do not even fear those who can kill the physical body. Take up your cross and follow the Christ.

People: Those who find their life will lose it, and those who lose their life for the sake of Christ will find it.

Leader: May the promises of God, the certainty of Christ, and the refreshing of the Holy Spirit sustain us until we meet again. Amen.

PROPER 8 · SUNDAY BETWEEN JUNE 26 AND JULY 2

Genesis 22:1–14
Psalm 13
Romans 6:12–23
Matthew 10:40–42

Call to Worship

Leader: We have been summoned by the Sovereign God Most High to offer our sacrifice.
People: Here I am, Lord.[54]
Leader: God demands that we bring our best to this time of worship.
People: Here I am, Lord.
Leader: The altar of devotion is prepared; God seeks a sinless offering.
People: Here I am, Lord. Use me in your service.
Leader: Let us worship the God who calls.
People: Amen.

Call to Confession

When God commands that we bring our most cherished possession and offer it in sacrifice, we try to hedge and dodge. We want to bring half-hearted service, less than honest commitment, and part-time worship. God will accept nothing less than our whole selves. Let us confess our sin before God, who continues to call and to wait.

Confession

God of Abraham and Isaac, we stand before your altar, trembling in fear. We know that you demand our best. It is so difficult to put it before you. For we never know what else you will require. Forgive us our sin. Help us to trust that you have already provided the most perfect sacrifice in your own son. Help us to know that your grace is sufficient before you call to us. In the name of the One who continues to call and to provide, we pray. Amen.

Words of Assurance

It is not the sacrifice that delights God, it is our willingness to return what has already been provided to us by God. When our will is submitted to God, the provision for what we need has been supplied. This is good news! Amen.

Responsive Reading Psalm 13

Leader: We continue to stand at the crossroads. God calls us to give and surrender when it seems as if we have already given enough. When will it be our turn to receive?

People: It seems as if God forgets about us. Sometimes we feel inconsequential and extremely insignificant.

Leader: The pain of waiting is difficult and the sorrow in our hearts is constant.

People: "How long will our enemies be exalted over us?" David cried this years ago and it remains our plea today.

Leader: It is such an honest feeling when it seems like hope is fading and the problems loom before us as pressing as ever.

People: God, hasten to our aid. The systems in place against us seem to have all the power. If we don't hear from you, our hope will fade and our spirits will fail within us.

Leader: We need a word from God! We need refreshing optimism to stir within us, in order that our enemies will not feel that they have the final word over our destiny.

People: We have watched the Liberator work in situations that were hard to call before. As we rehearse our story and remember our journey, the steadfast love of God has been a constant.

Leader: This strengthens our faith and brings joy to our hearts. We can sing unto this God who remains faithful.

Offertory Invitation

Jesus declares that whoever welcomes him also welcomes God who sent him. To receive Jesus is a free gift of love. As we share, we extend the welcome to others who need to come. Let us freely give.

Offertory Praise

Freely we have received and freely we have given. Gracious and Giving God, bless the givers and the gifts. You have promised to provide rewards equal to our sharing. For this we give you thanks. Amen.

Benediction

Leader: Leave! Know that you have been freed from sin.

People: Sin will not exercise its dominion in our mortal bodies. We have offered ourselves to God.

Leader: Leave! Know that you are not under the curse of the law, but that the grace of God abounds in you.

People: Thanks be unto God for the truth, which reigns in our hearts, freeing us from slavery to sin.

Leader: Leave! Walk in the knowledge of your eternal life.

People: For the wages of sin is death, but our free gift from God is eternal life in Christ Jesus our Sovereign. Amen.

PROPER 9 · SUNDAY BETWEEN JULY 3 AND JULY 9

Genesis 24:34–38, 42–49, 58–67
Psalm 45:10–17 or Song of Solomon 2:8–13
Romans 7:15–25a
Matthew 11:16–19, 25–30

Call to Worship

Leader: We gather in the name of the world's greatest love story.
People: We are children of love!
Leader: The journey of Isaac and Rebekah reminds us of how God leads us to love.
People: We are children of love!
Leader: God's love is tender, faithful, and forever springing up to bless us.
People: We are children of love!
Leader: The situations of our life have drawn us here; let us worship and be comforted by love!
People: Amen.

Call to Confession

Love calls out to us, seeks us, and tries to win us. But we hear other voices and stray far from home. Let us confess our sin, which blocks love and keeps us separate from God.

Confession

Lover of my soul, I do not understand my own actions. For I do not do what I want, but I do the very thing I hate . . . but in fact it is no longer I that do it, but sin that dwells in me. . . . So I find it to be a law that when I want to do what is good, evil lies close at hand. Wretched one that I am! Who will rescue me from this body of death? Thanks be to God through Jesus Christ our Lord. Forgive my sin, I want to be at home with love. Amen.

Words of Assurance

The good news is that the doors to love are always open and a welcome awaits all who seek to enter. Our confession and repentance allow us an honored reception as beloved children. Amen.

Responsive Reading Psalm 45:10–17

Leader: Listen and hear the music of rejoicing!

People: The sweet melodies of love call us by name.

Leader: The Companion of the ancestors woos us with sounds of pure delight.

People: Many other gods have sought our favors. They have tried to win our adoration with trinkets and novelties that would not last.

Leader: The enticements have been many and varied as they attempted to seduce us with vain charm.

People: But we remembered that we are adorned with the majestic kente cloth of a regal people.

Leader: The multicolored garments symbolize the great number of exalted and grand tribes from which we come.

People: With joy and with gladness we continue to be committed to the High God of the ancestors.

Leader: We are the offspring of an illustrious and noble people.

People: Our endeavors and contributions are heralded around the world.

Leader: The honor of God is celebrated in our lives.

People: The name of God is praised forever.

Offertory Invitation

All that we have is a generous gift from God. Now is the time when we can return a portion in gratitude and with thanks.

Offertory Praise

It is from your hand that we have received. It is from your strength that we have toiled. It is from your bounty that we share. May our gifts bless others, is our prayer. Amen.

Benediction

Leader: The invitation has been to come because we were weary and burdened.

People: In rehearsing the story we have received restoration.

Leader: The promise has been to take the yoke and learn about God for the comfort of our souls.

People: In remembering God's goodness our souls have been refreshed.

Leader: Go into the world, telling others about Love. The favor of God, the pardon of Christ, and the blessings of the Holy Spirit go before us.

People: Alleluia and amen.

PROPER 10 · SUNDAY BETWEEN JULY 10 AND JULY 16

Genesis 25:19–34 or Isaiah 55:10–13
Psalm 119:105–112 or Psalm 65:1–8, 9–13
Romans 8:1–11
Matthew 13:1–9, 18–23

Call to Worship

Leader: The Birthing God calls us to approach the fountain of life.
People: We come with anticipation to be part of the celebration
Leader: Many who have been barren will receive the blessing of creation here.
People: For the gift of God is the ability to bring to life more than human infants.
Leader: We are called to birth ideas, visions, and dreams for the continuation of God's world.
People: Our hearts are open to receive and to bring forth new life. Amen.

Call to Confession

When we have been barren and unfruitful, we often blame God. Yet birthing requires clean and wholesome conditions for survival. Let us confess the sin that stains our life and separates us from the God of Life.

Confession

Commencement of Existence, how often have we denied ourselves the opportunity to participate in life? We have remained on the fringes and neglected your call to bear fruit. Forgive us our sin. Fill us with the spirit of expectation, which can nourish and nurture the new life within us. Help us to conceive of your love and to struggle in earnest to be the bearers of your good news, we pray. Amen.

Words of Assurance

Rebekah, our foremother, was barren for many years, yet God blessed her womb and she birthed forth nations for the praise of God. God continues to answer our prayers and we can participate in the joy of new life. This is good news. Amen.

Responsive Reading Psalm 119:105–112

Leader: The Word of God has remained a nonflickering light for our journey.

People: The expression of truth has been the guide on our pilgrimage.

Leader: The pledge of the ancestors has bound us to the Utterance of Existence.

People: Despite affliction, persecution, and a difficult life, we have made covenant to be faithful to God.

Leader: Our lives are securely bound to the eternal.

People: We remain teachable and expectant, even when our praise is a great sacrifice.

Leader: We have had no easy journey and our lives are forever made more complex.

People: The systems of evil never take a break and entrapments are everywhere.

Leader: Yet we will not turn from following God.

People: Our ancestry provides a legacy of faith.

Leader: The deeds of God are established in our history.

People: We will rehearse, remember, and recall this tradition of faith, which will lead us into eternity.

Offertory Invitation

There is now no condemnation for those who are in Christ Jesus. For the law of the Spirit of Life in Christ Jesus has set us free from the law of sin and death. Let us share so that others might experience this great gift.

Offertory Praise

God, your Word declares that "anyone who does not have the Spirit does not belong to Christ." Receive our offerings so that others will hear and come to know and to receive the Spirit of God who raised Jesus from the dead and gives us an inheritance of eternal life. In the name of the Resurrected One, we pray. Amen.

Benediction

Leader: We have heard the words of life.

People: We have listened and received the seed.

Leader: Go! Bear the Word within you and give birth where ever you go.

People: The Word has fallen on good and fertile ground.

Leader: Leave with the understanding that you will bear fruit, some thirty, some sixty, and some even a hundredfold.

People: We leave as lights and lamps in a world that hungers for illumination.

Leader: The Word of God, the new life of Christ, and the refreshing winds of the Holy Spirit go before us.

People: Amen.

PROPER 11 · SUNDAY BETWEEN JULY 17 AND JULY 23

Genesis 28:10–19a or Isaiah 44:6–8
Psalm 139:1–12, 23–24 or Psalm 86:11–17
Romans 8:12–25
Matthew 13:24–30, 36–43

Call to Worship

Leader: Come, we who love God, and let our joys be known![55]
People: Surely the Sovereign God is in this place!
Leader: We have survived another week!
People: We have gathered for a fresh anointing of the Holy Spirit.
Leader: Lift up your heads, Oh ye gates. Be ye lifted up, ye everlasting doors.
People: The King of glory is here! How awesome is this place!
Leader: Oh, come let us adore him.[56]
People: He is Christ, the Lord! Amen.

Call to Confession

In the hustle and bustle of our lives, often we neglect spending quality time with God. Then there are those times when the presence of the Eternal is all around us, and in our spiritual blindness, we miss every sign. Yet this morning, we have another opportunity to be in contact with the Rock of Ages. Let us confess the sin in our lives, which separates us.

Confession

Liberating One, you have adopted us into your royal family and given us new hope. For in hope we are saved. We continue to fall back into old habits and relationships and live as debtors to our flesh. If we continue to live according to the desires of our flesh, we will die. Forgive us our sin. By the power of your Holy Spirit, put to death the appetite in us that sins against you and your holy Word. Lead us into wholeness, we pray. In the name of our Redeemer and Christ. Amen.

Words of Assurance

All who are led by the Spirit of God are children of God. For we did not receive a spirit of slavery to fall back into fear, but we have received a spirit of adoption. When we cry out in recognition of our relationship to the Creator, it is that very Spirit bearing witness with our spirit that we are children of God, and if children, then heirs of God and joint heirs with Christ—if, in fact, we suffer with him so that we may be glorified with him. And this, my sisters and brothers, is mighty good news! Amen.

Responsive Reading Psalm 139:1–12, 23–24

Leader: Exalted Inquisitor of Souls, your examination of us is thorough and intimate.
People: Search me, Jesus!
Leader: Our convenient lies and excuses do no good before you, since you read our thoughts.
People: Search me, Jesus!
Leader: Before a word of our meager rap is put in place, you have the inside story.
People: Search me, Jesus!
Leader: Your intense scrutiny is overwhelming, your knowledge of our intent staggering!
People: Search me, Jesus!
Leader: There is no hiding place from you. There is no spot that you are not!
People: Search me, Jesus!
Leader: In the ecstatic moments of our lives, you are present. When our failures are monumental, your constant presence is available.
People: Search me, Jesus!
Leader: Even the darkness is not dark to you; the night is as bright as the day, for darkness is as light to you.
People: Search me, Almighty Quest for Excellence! Point out the wickedness in my life and lead me in the way to you!

Offertory Invitation

Hope that is seen is not hope. Therefore, the just live by their faith. Let our faith in the Mystery of Hope stimulate our sharing. Far too many have no hope in our world.

Offertory Praise

All of creation waits with eager longing for the revealing of the children of God. Multiply these, our gifts, in the obtaining of freedom that the world might be bountiful. Amen.

Benediction

Leader: The whole world is our parish! Leave to spread good seeds.
People: We leave as children of God's realm to plant for the coming harvest.
Leader: The harvest is at the end of the age. Leave with the purpose of sowing in mind.
People: We leave to make a good crop for the Master! We are well aware of what is required!
Leader: The God of the field, the Sower of seed, and the Multiplier of the harvest, go before us.

PROPER 12 · SUNDAY BETWEEN JULY 24 AND JULY 30

Genesis 29:15–28 or 1 Kings 3:5–12
Psalm 105:1–11, 45b or Psalm 128 or Psalm 119:129–136
Romans 8:26–39
Matthew 13:31–33, 44–52

Call to Worship

Leader: Who will separate us from the love of Christ?
People: Will hardship, distress, persecution, famine, nakedness, peril, or death?
Leader: As it is written, "For your sake we are being killed all day long; we are accounted as sheep to be slaughtered."
People: No! In all these things we are more than conquerors through him who loves us.
Leader: For I am persuaded that neither death, nor life, nor angels, nor rulers.
People: Nothing that is present, nothing that is to come, not powers, nor heights, nor depths, nor anything else in all of creation will be able to separate us from the love of God in Christ Jesus our Lord. Amen.

Call to Confession

Sometimes scripture seems to mock our reality. We forget that what we see and hear is not the whole story. For the times we are separated from God by the sin of our lives, let us confess!

Confession

Spirit of Prayer, help us in our weakness. For we do not know how to pray as we ought, but the Holy Spirit intercedes for us with sighs too deep for words. When we consider that nothing can ever separate us from your love, we are sorry for the times we have simply walked away from you. Forgive us our sin. Search our hearts. Restore us to a right relationship with you, we pray. Amen.

Words of Assurance

The Holy Spirit intercedes for the saints according to the will of God. And we know that all things work together for good for those who love God. . . . Who is to condemn? It is Jesus Christ, who died, yes, who was raised, who is at the right hand of God, who indeed intercedes for us. This is good news! Amen.

Responsive Reading Psalm 105:1–11, 45b

Leader: Praise God, saints! God is good!

People: All the time!

Leader: And all the time.

People: God is good!

Leader: Let's give unto God the glory due the mighty acts that have preserved our lives.

People: Glory to God!

Leader: If you know God as a way-maker, you ought give up the praise.

People: God is worthy to be praised.

Leader: Let us sing unto the Lord a new song.

People: We lift the name of our God in high praise.

Leader: When I think of the goodness of our Lord, and all that has been done for us, my soul cries out in rejoicing.

People: Where would we be without the steadfast love of God?

Leader: When the road has been rough and the crowds have grown thin, the Lord remembered us and came to our defense.

People: Lift the Savior up!

Leader: When the mountains have been high and the valleys extremely low, it's been the Love of God who has enabled our journey.

People: From the promise made to our foreparents, in the Garden of Eden, God has been mindful of and faithful to every word of our covenant relationship.

Leader: An everlasting and eternal inheritance is our portion, if we will hold out and trust in the promises of God.

People: Our hope is anchored in the High God.

Offertory Invitation

The realm of God is like yeast that a woman took and mixed in with three measures of flour until all of it was leavened. That little portion multiplied into greatness. What we give to God will increase until the whole world comes to adore the Savior. Let's sow generously.

Offertory Praise

God, you take little and do much with it. You take the ordinary and perform the extraordinary through it. Receive these, our gifts, and use them to accomplish your purpose in the earth. In the name of the Tree of Life, we pray, with thanksgiving. Amen.

Benediction

Leader: Leave! Know that you are a great treasure.
People: We leave with gratitude for the Christ who gave his life to purchase our salvation.
Leader: Leave! Know that you are like a pearl of great value.
People: We leave knowing that our souls were valued by Jesus Christ.
Leader: Leave! Know that the love of God, the intercession of Christ, and the treasure of the Holy Spirit go before us into the world. Amen.

PROPER 13 · SUNDAY BETWEEN JULY 31 AND AUGUST 6

Genesis 32:22–31 or Isaiah 55:1–5
Psalm 17:1–7, 15 or Psalm 145:8–9, 14–21
Romans 9:1–5
Matthew 14:13–21

Call to Worship

Leader: This is the place of blessing! God is here!
People: We have been wrestling with issues of life, and oft times we are not sure that God knows our name.
Leader: God wants to change our names. For the old names represents old ways. Open yourself to a new touch and a new name.
People: This will require change and change hurts.
Leader: You might have to limp through life, but with God's blessings, your journey will be secure.
People: We come to worship the God who is present. Amen.

Call to Confession

The pain of people of color causes our hearts great sorrow. The many and diverse methods of oppression used against us is a source of unceasing anguish. For whenever people are denied their basic human rights it is sin. Yet we are people of the covenant. God is on our side. Let us confess the sin that separates us from our Help.

Confession

God of glory and God of power, it is to you that we look for help. The pain of our hearts has caused us to rely upon our own devices and to stray away from your love. Forgive us our sin. Restore us to right relationship with you. Shine in us so that others might see our adoption into your royal family. In the name of Grace, we pray. Amen.

Words of Assurance

To the people of God belong adoption, glory, covenants, worship, and promises; to them belong the patriarchs and matriarchs and from them, according to the flesh, comes the Messiah, who is over all and blessed by God forever. This is good news! Amen.

Responsive Reading Psalm 17:1–7, 15

Leader: Our hearts cry for freedom, liberty, and justice. God, hear our petitions.

People: We know our own sins and limitations, but we approach God with confession on our lips.

Leader: Laws have been written, traditions have been established, and customs have taken root that keep us denied our basic rights to human dignity and respect as people of God.

People: We know that God is watching. The walls of oppression, the past laws of apartheid, and the courts of injustice are being dismantled everywhere.

Leader: The dream of justice and the visions of shalom continue to visit us, even in the night.

People: When we are put to the test, God finds us faithfully waiting on the fulfillment of our destiny.

Leader: Regardless of what others resort to, we cannot turn to violence and hatred.

People: Our steps will hold steady to the ways of peace.

Leader: We will continue to call upon the name, the power, and the hope we have in God.

People: God does hear! God does answer! God does come!

Leader: The steadfast love of God is our only confidence.

People: In the shelter of God's love we take comfort.

Leader: When we see God face to face, it will be in victory, with songs of joy upon our lips.

People: When we see God, we will sing and shout—troubles over, burdens down—and we will study war no more!

Offertory Invitation

Give! And it shall be given unto you. Pressed down, shaken together, and running over, is the promise. Let's try God!

Offertory Praise

God, we offer our resources to you. Like the little lad, we want to share with others. Please accept our offerings. Bless them, multiply them, and use them for greater good in the world. In the name of sharing, we pray. Amen.

Benediction

Leader: Leave this place of blessing, comforted by the One who met us here.
People: We leave to continue the journey to wholeness.
Leader: Leave this place of name changing, assured that God goes before us.
People: We leave this place blessed with the name Love.
Leader: Leave this place of sharing, challenged to give what you have received.
People: We leave this place, willing to share what we have received.
Leader: Go in Grace, Power, and Security!
People: Amen and amen.

PROPER 14 · SUNDAY BETWEEN AUGUST 7 AND AUGUST 13

Genesis 37:1–4, 12–28 or 1 Kings 19:9–18
Psalm 105:1–6, 16–22, 45b or Psalm 85:8–13)
Romans 10:5–15
Matthew 14:22–33

Call to Worship

Leader: We gather to worship the God who is Love.
People: When our siblings hate us and refuse to accept our offerings of help, God's love sustains.
Leader: We gather to worship the God who is Deliverer.
People: When our lives are threatened, when pits are dug for our destruction, God's deliverance is steadfast.
Leader: We gather to worship the God who is Savior.
People: The world around us is changing and unstable. Yet, our God remains constant and unchanged. We offer worship to this Faithful God.

Call to Confession

As the world ages, the story of Joseph remains current and fresh. Hatred continues to rear its ugly head. And we often fall into its trap. Let's confess our sin.

Confession

God, the story of being sold into a strange land sounds so familiar to our ears. The pain of rejection and the reality of the pit is close to our hearts. We find it easy to hate and difficult to let go of our need for revenge. Forgive us our sin. Help us to remember that there is only one family and you are the refuge of us all. Let your gift of reconciliation work through us. In the name of Hope, we pray. Amen.

Words of Assurance

The Word is near you, on your lips and in your hearts. That is the Word of faith that we proclaim. If you confess with your lips that Jesus is Lord, and believe in your heart that God raised him from the dead, you will be saved. This is good news! Amen.

Responsive Reading Psalm 105:1–6, 16–22, 45b

Leader: It's testimony time! Surely there is a story in the house just waiting to be told.
People: Words are insufficient! Even music is inadequate to describe the miracles, the marvels, and the majestic works of God on our behalf.
Leader: We must tell it! Our full hearts of praise must be shared, as we give honor to our Bridge over Troubled Waters.
People: When our hope was faint, when our faith was faltering, and when all other resources failed, the Helper of the Helpless came to our aid.
Leader: How do we keep our memory strong? How do we preserve God's exploits for the sake of the generations to come?
People: We keep alive the stories of the matriarchs and patriarchs. We rehearse their deeds and recall the truth of their lives. We are their offspring. They live on in us.
Leader: The story of testing and trials, of mountains, valleys, and pits is not new to us. We have walked this road many times before.
People: The Supplier of Every Need has always sent before us those who found favor, became resourceful, and prepared the way for us.
Leader: God's ways are past our comprehension.
People: God's wisdom is handed down by the ancestors. For them, we offer God righteous and hearty praise.

Offertory Invitation

Everyone who calls on the name of the Christ shall be saved. But how are they to call on One in whom they have not believed? And how are they to believe in One of whom they have never heard? How are they to hear without someone to proclaim him? Our sharing promotes this good news of salvation. Let's share from thankful hearts.

Offertory Praise

Lavishly Generous God, you are gracious to all. May these, our gifts from you, be used to bless others, is our prayer. Amen.

Benediction

Leader: The winds and the waves will continue to threaten and even frighten us in the days to come.

People: But Christ has commanded that we have no fear.

Leader: The ghosts of dangers will continue to rise, causing us great anxiety.

People: But Christ has commanded that we have no fear.

Leader: We leave in the assurance of God's love, the confidence of Christ's command, and the power of the Holy Spirit.

People: Amen.

PROPER 15 · SUNDAY BETWEEN AUGUST 14 AND AUGUST 20

Genesis 45:1–15 or Isaiah 56:1, 6–8
Psalm 133 or Psalm 67
Romans 11:1–2a, 29–32
Matthew 15:10–20, 21–28

Call to Worship

Leader: The Preserver of Life has summoned us here.
People: Truly God is good to Zion. We have been spared.
Leader: The Planner of Destinies desires an audience with us.
People: Truly God is good to Zion! We have been delivered.
Leader: Weeping may endure for a night, but the joy of life now calls.
People: Truly God is good to Zion! We gather to worship and sing praise.

Call to Confession

In the divine design, even evil plots against us serve a higher purpose. Yet the human desire for revenge is strong and oft times we sin. Let us confess.

Confession

Reconciler of nations, your plan for life is so complex. We cannot begin to unravel the mysteries of our existence. Yet we are aware that you are in the intricate scheme. Forgive us our sins—those against others and those against you. In your name, we pray. Amen.

Words of Assurance

God longs to be in relationship with us. It is from God that we have received the ministry of reconciliation. With joy, let us return to this loving connection. Amen.

Responsive Reading Psalm 133

Leader: The Harambee is come! The connections of our ancestry are strengthening. Our roots are tangled. We are one family.

People: It is in our connecting, community, and sweet communion that God is honored and glorified.

Leader: Better than exquisite, dark, rich chocolates and more satisfying than a robust, sweet wine, is true Harambee. A united family brings a smile to the face of God.

Offertory Invitation

God has called us, a remnant on the earth. God has not rejected us but shown mercy in order that others might obtain mercy. In our sharing, the blessings of God are spread.

Offertory Praise

God, your gifts and calling are irrevocable. Let these, our gifts, help carry your call into all the world. Amen.

Benediction

Leader: Great faith has called us here.

People: The story of Joseph, his pit experience, and God's grace has encouraged us.

Leader: Great faith has called us here.

People: The story of the hurting woman and her daughter, delivered by our Wounded Healer, has consoled us.

Leader: Great faith has called us here.

People: The stories of our faith enfold us as we leave.

Leader: The God of our faith, the Christ of our courage, and the tenacity of the Holy Spirit go before us.

People: Amen.

PROPER 16 · SUNDAY BETWEEN AUGUST 21 AND AUGUST 27

Exodus 1:8–2:10 or Isaiah 51:1–6
Psalm 124 or Psalm 138
Romans 12:1–8
Matthew 16:13–20

Call to Worship

Leader: The time has come. The hour is at hand. The call to give birth is ours.
People: The political climate is against us. The economic situation is depressed. The heat is oppressive and this is not our time!
Leader: The spirits of Shiphrah and Puah live! We are called to be midwives for our own deliverance. The call to give birth is ours.
People: God blessed the midwives who were partners in building community. The people multiplied and became strong.
Leader: The time is come. The hour is at hand.
People: We bless the name of the Birthing God. Amen.

Call to Confession

I appeal to you, therefore, brothers and sisters, by the mercies of God, to present yourselves a living sacrifice, holy and acceptable to God, which is our spiritual worship. Let us confess our sin.

Confession

Emancipator of our souls, we have conformed to this world and bought into the lie of being like others. We have not sought your will, but have listened to the popular opinions of our day. Forgive us our sin. Help us to know and to live a life that is good, acceptable, and perfect in your sight. In the name of Wholeness, we pray. Amen.

Words of Assurance

Blessed be God! By our own confession, we have escaped the snare of the enemy. Our help is in the name of the Sovereign God. This is good news!

Responsive Reading Psalm 124

Leader: The witness of our lives, the survival of our culture, and the stories of our faith help us to know God's saving grace.
People: Great is our God and great is God's praise.
Leader: Our community has been assaulted on every front as excuses are made to exclude us from the centers of power.
People: Great is our God and great is God's praise.
Leader: We know the vast assortment of humiliation, complex schemes of seething anger, and slick political plots devised to marginalize us further.
People: Great is our God and great is God's praise.
Leader: The flood of hatred has not carried us away and the torrents of backlash will not be our demise.
People: Great is our God and great is God's praise.
Leader: Our defense is God. Our salvation is sure. Our deliverance is near!
People: Great is our God and great is God's praise.

Offertory Invitation

The wealth of the ages has been left in our hands. As faithful stewards, we are called to give in generous measure.

Offertory Praise

Generous God, you have given unto us the keys of the realm. We release our faith in your ability to take our little and multiply it for your use. Amen.

Benediction

Leader: We are the body of Christ;
People: We are members of one another.
Leader: We have gifts that differ.
People: We have the common grace of God.
Leader: Use your gifts to bring new life into the world.
People: We will be midwives of new life.
Leader: May the God of new life, the Christ of community, and the Spirit of renewal go before us!
People: Amen.

PROPER 17 · SUNDAY BETWEEN AUGUST 28 AND SEPTEMBER 3

Exodus 3:1–15 or Jeremiah 15:15–21
Psalm 105:1–6, 23–26, 45c or Psalm 26:1–8
Romans 12:9–21
Matthew 16:21–28

Call to Worship

Leader: Come ye, disconsolate,[57] The Seeing and Hearing God is present.
People: We have gathered to pause and to consider God.
Leader: Come ye, disconsolate, the Observing One has taken note of every misery.
People: We have set aside our labor to honor God.
Leader: Come ye, disconsolate, the Calling God is here.
People: "Here I am, Lord."[58] Use me in your service. Amen.

Call to Confession

We live in a society where exploitation and violence are both common and accepted. Yet God has called us to live in a counterculture where love is the ideal. Let us confess our sin.

Confession

Lover of the unlovable, we approach you in reverence and repentance. We have hated those who persecuted us and we have sought our own revenge. We have resented those who progressed more quickly and have cursed their seeming success. Forgive us our sin. Restore us to faithful living, we pray. Amen.

Words of Assurance

"Do not repay anyone evil for evil, but take thought of what is noble. If it is possible, live peaceably with all. Beloved, never avenge yourselves, but leave room for the wrath of God; for as it is written, 'Vengeance is mine, I will repay, says the Lord.'" This is the Word of our God. Amen.

Responsive Reading Psalm 105:1–6, 23–26, 45b

Leader: Exalt the name of our God. Lift high the praise of the Great I Am.
People: The music of falling barriers and the crescendo of ever-widening liberty rises in a symphony of awesome praise.
Leader: As God's people gain respect for their humanity in South Africa and the dance of freedom spreads across the world, even the angels join the "Alleluia Chorus."[59]
People: We are children of the diaspora, God's chosen ones, preserved and freed to actualize our potential.
Leader: We have been aliens in foreign lands, and God preserved our nation.
People: Today, our strength and courage are renowned. The hate we have endured has made us strong.
Leader: Many have been called by God to lead us to deliverance and wholeness. For their wisdom and determination, we praise the Lord!

Offertory Invitation

We are admonished to "Rejoice in hope, be patient in suffering, persevere in prayer. Contribute to the needs of the saints. . . ." Giving is a key practice of the community of the faithful. Let us practice what we preach.

Offertory Praise

God, you call us to live the abundant life, and from our abundance we have shared. May our living and our giving change the lives of others for your realm. In the name of Jesus Christ, we pray. Amen.

Benediction

Leader: You have been called to be followers of the Lamb.
People: We will deny ourselves, take up our cross, and follow the Christ.
Leader: If you want to save your life, lose it for the sake of the realm of God.
People: What would it profit us to gain the whole world and lose our life?
Leader: The Son of God will repay everyone for the deeds they have done. Be ready when he comes.
People: Amen and amen.

PROPER 18 · SUNDAY BETWEEN SEPTEMBER 4 AND SEPTEMBER 10

Exodus 12:1–14 or Ezekiel 33:7–11
Psalm 149 or Psalm 119:33–40
Romans 13:8–14
Matthew 18:15–20

Call to Worship

Leader: This is a day of new beginnings![60]
People: Thank God for the saving blood.
Leader: This is a call to active community.
People: Thank God for the redeeming blood.
Leader: This is our time of celebrating life.
People: Thank God for the renewing blood.
Leader: Death has passed over us.
People: We will remember and celebrate our salvation. Praise unto our God. Amen.

Call to Confession

We have become too singular in our thought. The deliverance of God's people has always been a community affair. The celebration of the Passover and the promise of new beginnings came to those willing to be involved in the lives of others. Whenever we deviate from God's ideal, it is sin. Let us pray.

Confession

Center of our joy, you have called us to "love one another." We have failed to obey your law. In our desire to live the "good life," we have become inwardly focused. We have neglected the care of others and have not loved our neighbors as we love ourselves. Forgive us our sin. Restore in us a sense of community and enlarge our hearts with love, we pray. Amen.

Words of Assurance

Where two or three of God's family are gathered, the presence of love is guaranteed! This is our salvation. Thanks be unto God. Amen.

Responsive Reading Psalm 149

Leader: Celebrate the Ultimate One! People of God, rejoice, for the Lion of the Tribe is glorious.

People: Let the young rappers create praise; call the liturgical dancers and let them bow and sway in delight of our Creator.

Leader: Let the choirs be jubilant and the instruments join in with festive sound.

People: For our God is a music maker, who called forth melody from wind, birds, and seas.

Leader: Celebrate the Creator of Life! Celebrate the Victorious Redeemer! Oh, come, let us adore our God.

People: We are the pleasure of the Holy One. This is reason alone to celebrate with praise.

Leader: Our task is not to seek vengeance on others, nor are we left to punish those who have inflicted needless pain in our lives.

People: High praise will execute judgement on those who have withheld justice and equality.

Leader: The faithfulness of God demands our praise.

People: We celebrate the Ultimate One.

Offertory Invitation

To withhold from our neighbors is to steal from the Giver of Life. To share from a loving heart satisfies the demands of a generous God.

Offertory Praise

The gift of life is reason enough to share our means. We have received so much from your bounty, Lavish God, until giving is simply our grateful response. Let our sharing love bless your world. Amen.

Benediction

Leader: Go into the world, reaching out to your neighbors.

People: We leave to be God's family.

Leader: Go into the world, loving your neighbor, as you love yourself.

People: We leave to be God's family.

Leader: Go into the world, celebrating life. The love of God, the unity of Christ, and the sweet communion of the Holy Spirit are ours!

People: Amen!

PROPER 19 · SUNDAY BETWEEN SEPTEMBER 11 AND SEPTEMBER 17

Exodus 14:19–31 or Genesis 50:15–21
Psalm 114 or Exodus 15:1b–11, 20–21 or Psalm 103:1–7, 8–13
Romans 14:1–12
Matthew 18:21–35

Call to Worship

Leader: The Pillar of cloud and fire invites our participation in worship.
People: We come with joy to meet the Sovereign of the universe.
Leader: We are called to stop and rest on our journey, to be refreshed along the way.
People: The noise of the enemy is so loud. The threat of destruction has wearied us, even in the night watch.
Leader: We are called to remember that seas become dry land and enemies will be destroyed.
People: Let's rehearse our faith stories and be reminded that we are yet in good hands! Praise unto the Delivering God. Amen.

Call to Confession

Loud noises from hate groups, terrifying movements of the unstable economic trends, and our fear of the unknown cause us to worry and to fret about the future. The same God who guided Israel through the wilderness into safety wants to lead us. Being afraid of enemies causes much of our sin. Let us confess.

Confession

Watcher for our souls, on you we call for forgiveness of our sin. We have doubted your ability to repeat your saving acts for us. We have tried to be our own savior. Forgive us. Lead us into the newness of life, which waits beyond our sea of anxious thought. Help us to walk behind you into tomorrow, we pray. Amen.

Words of Assurance

God welcomes all of us who are weak in faith. Our reception is based on our confession. And it is written that every knee shall bow and every tongue shall give praise to the One who saves. This is good news. Amen.

Responsive Reading Psalm 114

Leader: From Africa to America, we have emerged a people sustained by the Strong Hand.

People: Prior to our Middle Passage, across the raging sea, we have had sanctuary in the High God.

Leader: Walls have come down, strongholds have been broken, and we have been held secure.

People: We have scaled the mountains of inequity and been guided through the wilderness of injustice.

Leader: The presence of God is powerful among us.

People: The God who turns a watery grave into dry land continues to call us by name.

Offertory Invitation

The Scripture declares that we do not live unto ourselves. What we do and what we neglect to do affect the lives of many others. Let us be generous in our sharing with a world filled with diverse needs.

Offertory Praise

Purpose of Being, we offer to you our gifts. May they be a means to ensure that others might experience your new life. Amen.

Benediction

Leader: It is time to settle our accounts with God and with each other.

People: What do we owe for love, so divine?

Leader: We owe allegiance and commitment to our God.

People: What do we owe for love, so divine?

Leader: We owe forgiveness to those in the community of faith.

People: What do we owe for love, so divine?

Leader: You can never pay the amount that you owe!

People: How will we settle our account?

Leader: Be merciful and generous with others. Be forgiving and tender with those who belong to the realm of God. Let love work in you.

People: With the love of our God, the redemptive work of Christ, and the power of the Holy Spirit, we can leave, knowing that our accounts are paid in full. Amen.

PROPER 20 · SUNDAY BETWEEN SEPTEMBER 18 AND SEPTEMBER 24

Exodus 16:2–15 or Jonah 3:10–4:11
Psalm 105:1–6, 37–45 or Psalm 145:1–8
Philippians 1:21–30
Matthew 20:1–16

Call to Worship

Leader: The stuff we engage in all week long does not feed the deep hungers of our souls. So the Manna of Heaven longs to feed us today.
People: Feed us until we want no more.
Leader: The grumbling and murmuring of our hearts stems from our searching for a way out of the wilderness.
People: Feed us until we want no more.
Leader: The Bread of Life invites us to eat until we want no more.
People: Rain from Above, feed us and we will offer you praise. Amen.

Call to Confession

"Draw near to the God of the Ages" is our scriptural invitation. And we seek to find our satisfaction in everything else. Our refusal to eat of the Sustenance of the World is sin. Let us confess together.

Confession

God of plenteous bounty, we come to you in repentance of our sin. We have grumbled and complained about the choices we have made in our lives. We have been lost in the wilderness of our own sin. Now, our hungers have gotten worse and the pain of emptiness is great within us. Forgive us our sin and feed us with the Bread of Life. In the name of the Banquet of Glory, we pray. Amen.

Words of Assurance

Living our lives in a manner that is worthy of the gospel of Christ calls us to stand firm in the profession of our faith. The power of the Holy Spirit works within us to bring us to fullness of joy. This is God's doing and it's a marvel in our eyes. This is good news. Amen.

Responsive Reading Psalm 105:1–6, 37–45

Leader: Oh, give thanks to the Doer of Great Deeds. Tell the world what has been done for you.

People: The goodness of God swells up within us. The exploits done on our behalf convince us that miracles yet occur.

Leader: Give thanks for the Strength of the Ages, who is with us continually.

People: We glory in the accomplishments of our past, for we know God is with us.

Leader: We are the offspring of greatness. The seeds of destiny are within us.

People: Majestic worth has been deposited in us. Our value far exceeds the combined riches of the world.

Leader: The enemies of the cross have watched our forward advance with trepidation and uncertainty.

People: We have had the Guide of the journey with us both in good times and in bad. We have been cared for in every situation.

Leader: With the rise of every sun and the shining of new moons we know the assurance of providential guardianship.

People: Food has always been provided and our thirst has been satisfied.

Leader: We have taken the least things and made them delights to the tongues.

People: Ways have been made where no escape seemed possible and even our desert experiences have blossomed into fruitful instruction.

Leader: The Word of God stands secure, and God's promises to the ancestors remain in force.

People: This calls for songs of joy. We, the descendants of a mighty heritage, will sing with ecstasy.

Leader: The wealth of the world is ours. It belongs to those who will possess the land.

People: The promised land is here. The victory is already won. Don't wait until the battle is over; shout now! Praise unto our Regal Head.

Offertory Invitation

We are called into the vineyard to labor and are paid a just wage. In order that others might come and share, we are invited to give.

Offertory Praise

God, it has been of your generosity that we have returned. May the labors of our hands help to call other laborers into your realm. Amen.

Benediction

Leader: Go into the world to work.
People: With serving hearts we leave.
Leader: Go into the world to sing new songs of joy.
People: With thankful hearts we leave.
Leader: Go into the world to tell of God's majestic deeds.
People: With the story upon our lips we leave.
Leader: The grace of God, the peace of Christ, and the power of the Holy Spirit go with us. Amen!

PROPER 21 · SUNDAY BETWEEN SEPTEMBER 25 AND OCTOBER 1

Exodus 17:1–7 or Ezekiel 18:1–4, 25–32
Psalm 78:1–4, 12–16 or Psalm 25:1–9
Philippians 2:1–13
Matthew 21:23–32

Call to Worship

Leader: Come, all who are disconsolate, the Encourager of Hearts is ready for you.
People: The news media gives such stark predictions and the naked eye sees little that is promising.
Leader: The mind of God is here to give you comfort from the pains inflicted by daily living.
People: We want to see the glory of the High Authority whose name is exalted in all the earth. We need to be touched by this Power Divine.
Leader: Come, beloved, with joy and delight, for all that we need is in Christ. God is at work in us, enabling us to both desire and perform exploits in the world.
People: We come, with joy to share in the wonders of the Holy Spirit, to confess our needs before God, and to give glory to the Christ of Calvary.

Call to Confession

The day is coming soon when every tongue shall confess that Jesus is Lord to the glory of God. To be prepared for that great day, we are called to work out our own salvation with fear and trembling. When we sin, confession is our road back to God. Let us pray.

Confession

Water of Life, flow within us and among us. We, like the children of Israel, are guilty of quarreling and complaining. Like them, we have wondered and questioned, "Is the Lord among us or not?" Many times we have not wanted to see you to acknowledge your requirements for right living. Often we are thirsty, and we go to various people and places seeking to satisfy the cravings of our souls. Forgive us our sin. Lead us to the Rock that satisfies and provides eternal life, we pray. Amen.

Words of Assurance

Even in our deserts of sin, the love of God provides for our restoration. This is good news. Amen.

Responsive Reading Psalm 78:1–4, 12–16

Leader: The hour of instruction has arrived. The school of life is in session.

People: Our lessons in life have been difficult to master. Our ancient history, of being despised and rejected because of being who God created, seems to never improve.

Leader: The difficulty often comes when we try to discern what is the truth of our history. There are many versions and we need to teach the valid claims of our ancestry.

People: Our children continue to search for their roots. The dances and hair styles all seek to identify with the marvelous stories of our past. They have heard that there was a time when our people could fly!

Leader: We cannot hide their history and we need to prepare them for their destiny.

People: Our legacy has accomplishments that astonish and provide evidence of daring feats of deliverance by God.

Leader: The journey from greatest to slavery and from slavery to a second elevation has been chronicled by our lives. The Strong Hand of the Universe has encompassed our pilgrimage and led us all the way.

People: The Maker of Ways has opened doors of opportunity, which give credit to our phenomenal rise. We will tell the stories and keep our history alive.

Offertory Invitation

We are instructed not simply to be concerned with what is important to our lives alone, but we are to be involved in the affairs of those in the faith community. The opportunity to share is ours.

Offertory Praise

We cannot pay for love divine. We cannot begin to calculate what we owe for your providence. So it is with apprehension that we offer gifts to you, Ultimate One. Accept these tokens of our appreciation and gratitude. Amen.

Benediction

Leader: Go into the world knowing that the power to accomplish is yours.
People: We leave confident that wonder-working power resides in us.
Leader: Go into the world knowing that the power to fly is yours.
People: We leave with the assurance that the Power of the Ages will lift us to the heights.
Leader: Go into the world knowing that the power to be change agents is yours.
People: We leave with the God of creation, the Christ of new life, and the Holy Spirit's ability working in us and on our behalf. Amen and amen.

PROPER 22 · SUNDAY BETWEEN OCTOBER 2 AND OCTOBER 8

Exodus 20:1–4, 7–9, 12–20 or Isaiah 5:1–7
Psalm 19 or Psalm 80:7–15
Philippians 3:4b–14
Matthew 21:33–46

Call to Worship

Leader: The "I Am" of the ages demands our presence.
People: We have come for Sabbath rest and re-creation.
Leader: We have had six days of labor and toil; it's time to adore Life.
People: Living Presence, speak to us and we will listen. Voice of
Existence, we need to hear from you.
Leader: Orderer of Our Steps, open unto us your Word of life.
People: We have come to worship and to offer praise. Amen.

Call to Confession

At all times and in every place we are to acknowledge the Sovereign One.
Our neglect is sin. Let us pray.

Confession

God, we come with bowed heads and humbled hearts. We ask forgiveness
for our sin. What you have required of us, we have neglected to do. What
you have commanded that we not do, we have done. The problem is the
sin that is in us. We have been too confident in our ability to make the
proper decisions for our lives without honoring you. Lover of our souls,
we recognize how far we have removed ourselves from you. We long for
harmony with you. Restore us. In the name of Christ we pray. Amen.

Words of Assurance

We are called now to forget the sin that lies behind us. Let us press on toward the goal, in order to gain the prize of God, who is Jesus. This is good
news. Amen.

Responsive Reading Psalm 19

Leader: Look around you. There is evidence everywhere that the God of creation is present.

People: From the rising of the sun, to the gentle breezes of the air, the singing of the birds and the colors changing in the trees, we know that the Architect of Beauty lives.

Leader: Words are not adequate, but with our eyes we can hear the majesty of the Divine Designer.

People: Deeds of wonder and echoes of thundering victories give credence to the Name Above All Names in the earth.

Leader: We are encompassed with signs of care. There is no place where God is absent. In the political area and the academic halls, in the chambers of injustice and the streets of mean ghettos, we can see clues pointing to God.

People: The Maker of Miracles always sends the winds of change and the elements of refreshment to our souls.

Leader: The simplicity of God's reality often amazes us. We want to see God as complex, technical, and modern.

People: Yet the unlearned and unlettered saw God. The inarticulate spoke of the Unknown. The infants in knowledge gave profound testimony to the genesis.

Leader: The reverence of timelessness is as old as creatures. Our first parents stood in awe of origin.

People: The Dew of Beginning and the Fresh Breath of Dawn continue to reverberate in us.

Leader: The Desire of Every Nation is sweeter than honey in the comb.

People: The Pillar and Ground of Truth is more valuable than the combined worth of every precious metal.

Leader: Being in union with God brings us great rewards. We remain alive and filled with viability for both today and tomorrow.

People: Keep us from falling away from the paths established by the ancestors. Keep us from the failure to remember whose we are.

Leader: Walk on by faith each day.

People: May the words of our mouths and the meditations of our hearts be acceptable unto our Rock and our Redeemer.

Offertory Invitation

For who we are, from where we have been brought, and for how we have been preserved, let us share our blessings.

Offertory Praise

God, you have given us all. We have been the recipients of your great grace and we continue to be amazed. Accept our offerings of thanksgiving and use them to bless your world. Amen.

Benediction

Leader: Go to be the people of God.
People: The wonders of God compel us.
Leader: Go to be the Church of God.
People: The Chief Cornerstone undergirds us.
Leader: Go to be fruitful in the world.
People: The Creativity of the Ages, the Christ of victory, and the power of the Holy Spirit are ours. Amen.

PROPER 23 . SUNDAY BETWEEN OCTOBER 9 AND OCTOBER 15

Exodus 32:1–14 or Isaiah 25:1–9
Psalm 106:1–6, 19–23 or Psalm 23
Philippians 4:1–9
Matthew 22:1–14

Call to Worship

Leader: People of God, this is our festival for the Divine One.
People: We have brought our money, our positions, and our titles to pay homage to the One Above All.
Leader: Your wealth and trinkets dishonor the God who delivers and saves.
People: But these things are important to us! We have offered ourselves as sacrifices to get the things that we own.
Leader: You have made your money, your positions, and your titles your gods. They cannot help you in distress or deliver you from your sin.
People: Golden calves have always been attractive and gotten us into trouble with the Eternal.
Leader: God remains steadfast, even in our foolishness. Enter into worship and give glory to God, saints.
People: Alleluia and amen.

Call to Confession

Trinkets have a way of taking possession of our lives. They take our eye off the Prize. Let us confess our sin.

Confession

God of the heavens, forgive us for allowing created things to move us from worship of you. We are guilty of wanting to see, handle, and manipulate the little gods of our lives. We can feel powerful and be in control. But life always brings us a wake-up call. While our icons are flashy and attractive, they are not sufficient in the times of difficulty and stress. It is then that we find ourselves returning to the Reality who has sustained generations of ancestors. Once again, we come. We are knee bent and body bowed, for we need your mercy and grace to deliver us from our sin. In the name of Jesus Christ, we pray. Amen.

Words of Assurance

Beloved, whatever is true, whatever is honorable, whatever is just, whatever is pure, whatever is pleasing, whatever is commendable, if there is any excellence, and if there is anything worthy of praise, think about these things. Keep on doing the things that you have learned and received and heard and seen in the lives of saints. And the God of peace will be with you. This is good news.

Responsive Reading Psalm 106:1–6, 19–23

Leader: Blessings and honor to the Ancient of Days, whose steadfast love is legend.

People: From generation to generation, we have tried to recount the many and various ways that the Wonderful One has interceded on our behalf.

Leader: The deeds have been left on walls, written on papyrus scrolls, copied, translated, transcribed, handed down orally, and stored for posterity. But we have only scratched the surface of publishing the good news.

People: The justice of God has sustained us and the mercy of God has been our security.

Leader: Whenever the downtrodden and oppressed are lifted anywhere, we know that the High God remembers our plight.

People: We see the goodness of God made evident in the life of our children. The legacy of relationship continues. We glory in manifest love.

Leader: How horrible are the ways we have failed the Almighty. By both intentional and unintentional ways, we have sinned and been found among the evildoers.

People: We have even imitated our oppressors and worshiped their little gods.

Leader: All that the Living One has done for us was minimized by our actions.

People: We forgot the God of our ancestors. We walked away from the Help of the Ages.

Leader: Destruction should have been our fate. But somebody prayed for us. The prayers of the righteous have caused our redemption. God is faithful and just.

Offertory Invitation

Many have struggled and sacrificed to preserve for us this community of faith. Let us join with the believers and show our devotion.

Offertory Praise

Giver of Gifts, we long to be loyal companions in the work of ministry. Receive now the labor of our hands and use it to increase your realm. Amen.

Benediction

Leader: The wedding banquet has been spread.
People: We were invited to come and to dine.
Leader: Many have refused the gracious invitation.
People: We will go into the community and invite others to come.
Leader: Go, with the call of God, the supper of God's Son, and the power of the Holy Spirit.
People: We gladly leave, knowing that many are called, but few are chosen. Amen.

PROPER 24 · SUNDAY BETWEEN OCTOBER 16 AND OCTOBER 22

Exodus 33:12–23 or Isaiah 45:1–7
Psalm 99 or Psalm 96:1–9, 10–13
1 Thessalonisans 1:1–10
Matthew 22:15–22

Call to Worship

Leader: Come, all who are disconsolate and weary. The One who knows you by name is calling today.
People: We are weary of life and the struggle to survive.
Leader: You have found favor with the Holy One. Restoration and healing are present today.
People: We need to feel God's presence and to know God's glory.
Leader: God is here and will be gracious and generous.
People: We have come to offer praise and worship to the Merciful and Beneficent One. Amen.

Call to Confession

We have been called to a place in God where we would be covered by God's hand. Yet we have tried to find other places, away from God. Our seeking of other gods is sin. Let us confess.

Confession

"Rock of Ages, cleft for me, let me hide myself in thee."[61] How comforting the words of our ancestors' songs. Yet we have tried to run away from this close relationship with the Holy. It is uncomfortable to be watched so closely. It is uncanny to be known so intimately. It is unnerving to have our intents revealed. So we have tried to escape and we have sinned. Forgive us our sin. Be our Rock and our Security. We pray, in the name of our Redeemer. Amen.

Responsive Reading Psalm 99

Leader: The "I Am" is in charge!

People: Political figures tell us that they have the power.

Leader: The Rock of Ages is yet secure.

Leader: The media believes it has the authority to make reality.

People: The Eye of Infinity sees farther and knows better.

Leader: Our God is an awesome God![62]

People: We exalt the Lover of Justice.

Leader: Praise is due the Everlasting.

People: History has proven that many individuals come upon the stage of life. They make their contributions and are gone.

Leader: Yet there is One who is over all.

People: From generation to generation the Name Above Names has stood.

Leader: All flesh is temporary and their deeds are never permanent.

People: But the works of God's hand are established in creation.

Leader: The decrees of God are written into eternity.

People: Praise and honor, glory and dominion are due the Everlasting.

Offertory Invitation

The Word of God has sounded forth in every place. So that this Word of faith might be spread with power and authority, it is our privilege to share.

Offertory Praise

We give thanks to you, God, always remembering your steadfast love and continuing mercy unto us. Receive now the gifts of our labor and use it that others may be blessed. Amen.

Benediction

Leader: Grace to you, and peace.

People: We depart to serve the world.

Leader: Go. Let your lives proclaim the true and living God.

People: We have been chosen to be witnesses.

Leader: The call of God, the authority of Christ, and the power of the Holy Spirit go with you.

People: Amen.

PROPER 25 · SUNDAY BETWEEN OCTOBER 23 AND OCTOBER 29

Deuteronomy 34:1–12 or Leviticus 19:1–2, 15–18
Psalm 90:1–6, 13–17 or Psalm 1
1 Thessalonians 2:1–8
Matthew 22:34–46

Call to Worship

Leader: The Caller of the Redeemed says "Come to this mountain."
People: We come with expectant hearts to find counsel that will lead us.
Leader: The Mighty God, doer of exploits, says, "Come to this mountain."
People: We come with uplifted cups, wanting to be filled.
Leader: The Commander of the Host says, "Come to this mountain."
People: This is the mountain of God. The faithful have assembled to offer sacrifices of praise. Amen.

Call to Confession

Moses went to the mountain and saw the promised land. But due to unfaithfulness in one aspect of his life, he could not enter into the new land. Our unfaithfulness separates us from the promises of God. Let us confess the sin that blocks our relationship. Let us pray.

Confession

Unequaled Sovereign, we have seen the signs and wonders that testify to your providential care. We have witnessed your hand, guiding us through wilderness experiences. We know that you continue to make ways out of no ways. Yet we have been unfaithful to you. What you have told us to do, we have left undone. What you have told us to leave alone, we have wholeheartedly embraced. Forgive us our sin. We have come to your holy mountain to hear anew the instructions for our salvation. Anoint our ears, our eyes, and our hearts to your ways. In the name of Christ, we pray. Amen.

Words of Assurance

We have been approved by God to be entrusted with the message of the gospel. We are to live and to speak so that we please God, who tests our hearts. Our confessions please God and restore us to faithful living. This is our good news. Amen.

Responsive Reading Psalm 90:1–6, 13–17

Leader: God has been our place of refuge down through the generations.
People: Before the cosmos was interrupted by thought and emptiness gave way to fullness, there was the Supreme Reality.
Leader: We are less than a breath away from our destruction, for life issues forth each one.
People: Time is precious to us, for we count in terms of seconds and minutes. However, all time belongs to the Eternal.
Leader: It is foolish for us to waste the moments that we have been given. Senseless violence, wanton killings, and abuse of our bodies are thieves.
People: Drive-by shootings and gang violence must be stopped. Before they have an opportunity to begin living, many of our youth are destroyed.
Leader: Compassion of the Ages, have mercy on us.
People: Teach us how to return to the haven of your love so that we may pass love on.
Leader: The last two generations have lost their sense of direction. They are wandering, lost, and in seeming despair. Help us to reclaim our heritage.
People: Their hopelessness causes us much pain. We want to see them whole.
Leader: Let love be multiplied in us. Let us love them back into your security.
People: Faithful One, bless us.
Leader: Let the words of our mouths match the work of our hands so that we may talk the talk and walk the walk.
People: The evidence of our joyful and faithful living will win the lost souls.

Offertory Invitation

You shall love the Lord your God with all your heart, and with all your soul, and with all your mind. This is the greatest and first commandment. And you shall love your neighbor as yourself. On these two command-ments hang all the law and the prophets. Let us give out of our love.

Offertory Praise

God, you are our witness that neither words of flattery nor acts of greed separate us from you. But out of our sincere desire to love you and our neighbor, we openly share what we have received. Bless both givers and receivers, we pray. Amen.

Benediction

Leader: Go! With courage in your hearts to serve God and neighbor.
People: We leave to follow Christ.
Leader: Go! As witnesses of mountaintop experiences, proclaiming the Mystery.
People: We leave to speak for Christ.
Leader: Go! Carrying a message of hope and reconciliation.
People: We leave as ambassadors of the cross.
Leader: The wisdom of God, the redemption of Christ, and the power of the Holy Spirit go before us. Amen.

PROPER 26 . SUNDAY BETWEEN OCTOBER 30 AND NOVEMBER 5

Joshua 3:7–17 or Micah 3:5–12
Psalm 107:1–7, 33–37 or Psalm 43
1 Thessalonians 2:9–13
Matthew 23:1–12

Call to Worship

Leader: The living God commands an audience with you.
People: We have answered the call on our lives.
Leader: You are the ones commanded to bear Christ in the arks of your hearts.
People: With this awesome responsibility, we have drawn near to hear the Word of God.
Leader: Without fail God will speak today.
People: Speak to our hearts, Bread of Life. We need a fresh Word. We come with acts of worship and praise. Amen.

Call to Confession

The waters of life continue to be stormy and tempestuous. They are seldom calm and demure. But the Ruler of the oceans and the seas is yet in control. Let us confess our sin to the One who continues to hear our feeble cries.

Confession

Prince of Peace, speak to the roaring tides of our lives. The winds and the waves of torment have driven us far from you. Forgive us our sin and speak peace to our souls. The loudness of many elements have caused us to neglect seeking the solace we can find in you. In this time and in this place, befriend us, we pray. Amen.

Words of Assurance

What a friend we have in Jesus, all of our sin and griefs to bear! What a privilege it is to carry everything to God in prayer![63] This is good news! Amen.

Responsive Reading Psalm 107:1–7, 33–37

Leader: It's time to affirm just how good God has been unto us. Somebody needs to be encouraged. Somebody needs to be uplifted. Somebody needs to know that God really does care.

People: There are witnesses from every corner of the world. There are those of us present from every area of this community. Whether from near or far, we can testify to the goodness of our Sovereign God.

Leader: Troubles and despair try to take our testimonies. Seeing the devastation in every part of the world and in our own community causes many to doubt.

People: But in the midst of every situation the Hand of Help is present.

Leader: Many of us have wandered in the wilderness of sin, lost and filled with overwhelming depression. Many of us have felt like giving up.

People: Evil is aloose everywhere. When we move away from the Bread of Life and neglect to drink from the Water That Satisfies, we will starve.

Leader: But, there is a Rock in the weary land, there is a Shelter in the time of storm and there is Bread for the hungry and Wine without end.

People: The Hope of the hopeless is here to feed our souls. The dry and parched soul will be restored and renewed. This is holy ground.

Leader: The Final Word speaks and calls us to eat until we are satisfied.

People: The table of life is set before us. We are home.

Leader: Eat and return to witness to new life and resurrection in the midst of seeming death.

People: We will be the fruitful fields. We will be the glorious vineyards. Our lives will produce an abundant yield.

Offertory Invitation

We have been called without price into this realm of glory. In our giving we show thanks to God.

Offertory Praise

Worthy One, we want to live a life that is pleasing in your sight. We want our conduct to always be pure, upright, and blameless before you. Accept the work of our hands as evidence of our love for you. Amen.

Benediction

Leader: Leave to practice what you have heard.

People: We go to live the gospel in our daily lives.

Leader: Leave to be instructors of others by your behaviors.

People: We go to witness that Christ is alive in us.

Leader: The greatest among you shall be servant of all.

People: As God in Christ came to serve us, we leave to serve others in the world.

Leader: The grace of God, the compassion of Christ, and the authority of the Holy Spirit go before us. Amen.

PROPER 27 . SUNDAY BETWEEN NOVEMBER 6 AND NOVEMBER 12

Joshua 24:1–3a, 14–25 or Amos 5:18–24
Psalm 78:1–7 or Psalm 70
1 Thessalonians 2:9–12
Matthew 25:1-13

Call to Worship

Leader: The Covenant God demands our attention.
People: The hungry have gathered to feast.
Leader: The Lamb of Calvary commands that we come.
People: The table is set before us.
Leader: The Comforter is here to minister.
People: With thirsty souls we come to worship and to praise. Amen.

Call to Confession

We have promised to serve the Lord, our God, to listen to and obey the commandments. We have promised to never forsake God, to honor and to follow with joy. We are promise breakers. Let us confess our sin.

Confession

Covenant Maker and Covenant Keeper, you have told us that you were a jealous God. It was your grace and your mercy that brought us and our ancestors from captivity and enslavement. You have done great exploits on our behalf. You have never broken the promise of the covenant. We are covenant makers and covenant breakers. We have made covenant with you and not kept faithful to our pledge of loyalty. Forgive us our sin. In the name of the covenant, we pray. Amen.

Words of Assurance

God's Word is established in the covenant. The Word is alive and cannot fail. The Word became flesh and lived among us. Now, it is our privilege to teach our children and our children's children about this awesome relationship with the Divine. This is good news. Amen.

Responsive Reading Psalm 78:1–7

Leader: Tell the stories of the ancestors and their relationship with the Ancient of Days.

People: Teach the history, recall the deeds, recount our legacy with the Supreme.

Leader: It is no secret what God will do! The accounts are too numerous to detail. From the days of old, before tape recorders and boom boxes, the stories were interwoven into the fabric of our lives.

People: Everybody needs to know about the God of All Colors.

Leader: We will teach our children the achievements of the elders; we will ensure that they know their roots.

People: The ancestors told us the narratives of exploits and deliverance.

Leader: The chronicles of the tribe are legendary.

People: The covenant of God, from the beginning, stands secure today.

Leader: Each generation is responsible for making the story relevant and real to the hearers. Each generation is mandated to keep the hope alive. Each generation must remember the story.

People: May the blood in our veins run dry, may the tongues of our mouth be turned to dust, may the brains of our mind be transformed into rot if we forget our origin and walk away from the Covenant Keeper.

Offertory Invitation

We are mandated to keep hope alive. We are commanded to share the story with a needy world. We are privileged to share. Let's give from grateful hearts.

Offertory Praise

Giver of gifts, we believe that Jesus died and rose again for our redemption and for the salvation of the whole world. What a joy it is to offer back to you a portion of what we've been blessed with. Truly, we are much obliged. Amen.

Benediction

Leader: Be ready! For we know not the day or the hour when the Bridegroom shall return.

People: Our lamps are trimmed and burning. Once again we have been satisfied with the anointing oil.

Leader: Be ready! For we know not the time nor the place when the bride of Christ shall be called for the marriage.

People: We are awake and alert. We are fed and refreshed. We are prepared to meet the Christ of glory.

Leader: The Holy One sustain you, the peace of Christ secure you, and the Holy Spirit empower your every day. Amen.

PROPER 28 · SUNDAY BETWEEN NOVEMBER 13 AND NOVEMBER 19

Judges 4:1–7 or Zephaniah 1:7, 12–18
Psalm 123 or Psalm 90:1–8 (9–11), 12
1 Thessalonians 5:1–11
Matthew 25:14–30

Call to Worship

Leader: Beloved, the time has come for worship!
People: How good and how pleasant it is to be in the house of God.
Leader: All week long we have lingered in places where evil reigned.
People: All week long we have endured the lies and half-truths told as reality.
Leader: Today, we are awake and sober, ready to hear a fresh word from the Living One.
People: Praise and worship, glory and honor is due the God of Integrity.

Call to Confession

During the week, it is easy to forget who is actually in charge of our lives. We live in a world where the false message is preached that we have to take care of ourselves. The truth is that God is always near to lead and to guide us in every step of our lives. When we go our own way it is sin. Let us confess the sin in our lives.

Confession

Watching Sovereign, we try so hard to look out for ourselves. We try to cover our own backs and to watch for signs of approaching danger. Often, in our attempts to observe the current trends, we forget about you. Forgive us our sin. Help us to always be alert to your presence and to your care. Give us the boldness to be attentive for your closeness, and the courage to see you in all of our times. In the name of the Alert God, we pray. Amen.

Words of Assurance

It is no secret what God can do! And what has been done for others continues to be done on our behalf. For God has not designed that we have to fight battles by ourselves. But through the work of Christ on Calvary, the victory is already ours! This is mighty good news. Amen.

Responsive Reading Psalm 123

Leader: The Warrior of the Universe sits on the throne of the cosmos, keenly aware of every situation.
People: For so many years we have looked to others for liberation. For too many years we have waited on others to make us free. Now, we turn our eyes toward the dawning of a new day. We can see clearly now! Our deliverance has always been in the mind of the Almighty.
Leader: It is grace and mercy that has sustained us until this day. We live each moment abundant in pardon and free of condemnation.
People: There are many who have planned our extinction. The warmongers have sought our total demise. Yet Great Help is always near us.

Offertory Invitation

Whether one talent, two, or five, we are to give according to our abilities. To do less is to rob the Giver of Every Good Gift.

Offertory Praise

Abundant Provider, we give you thanks for the results of our labor that we can share to help your realm increase. May your generosity bless ours, even a hundredfold, we pray. Amen.

Benediction

Leader: Stay awake and be sober. Do not fall asleep as you go.
People: We belong to the One Who Watches. Our spirits are alert.
Leader: Clothe yourself with the breastplate of faith and love, for you return to a hostile world.
People: We leave, assured by our hope of salvation in Jesus Christ.
Leader: Encourage one another and build each other up as you go. The battles do not belong to you. The conflicts of our lives belong to God.
People: Blessed assurance![64] What a friend we have in Jesus![65]
Leader: Go in the strength of God, the hope of Christ, and the joy of the Holy Spirit. Amen.

PROPER 29 · THE REIGN OF CHRIST

Ezekiel 34:11–16, 20–24 or Ezekiel 34:11–16, 20–24
Psalm 100 or Psalm 95:1–7a
Ephesians 1:15–23
Matthew 25:31–46

Call to Worship

Leader: The Shepherd of our souls bids us to gather.
People: From our scattered places and rambling thoughts we come to hear the Voice That Soothes.
Leader: All who hunger and are thirsty will be fed. All who are wounded and battle-scarred shall be healed.
People: The Monarch of Creation longs to attend to our needs.
Leader: The lost are welcome, and those who have strayed are sought. Every injury shall be addressed. And the weak will be strengthened.
People: This is Christ, our Potentate. We have come to offer our praise.

Call to Confession

We want to be the kings of our own castles and the captains of our own ships. But our castles are crumbling and our ships have gone astray. There is only One who can rule with justice. There is only One who can steer us into the light. When we seek to govern our own lives, it is sin. Let us confess.

Confession

Ruler of heaven and earth, we bow before your majesty. Earthly kings have given us such a pitiful portrait of your divine order. We have sought to move away from being controlled or led by human dictate, and in so doing we have run away from you. Forgive us our sin. Lead us into the pastures where our souls might be restored. The realm and the glory belong to you. In the name of Health, we pray. Amen.

Words of Assurance

God has spoken. The Word has been decreed. The Good Shepherd will lead us. Goodness and mercy shall follow us. And we shall dwell in the new realm for all of eternity. This is good news. Amen.

Responsive Reading Psalm 100

Leader: Crank up the volume. Turn up the decibels. For our rejoicing needs to be carried far and near. We have been kept alive. This is reason to celebrate.

People: Adoration is in order. For glad hearts have received the news of salvation. Lift up weary heads. Straighten up tired backs. Help is in the house!

Leader: Deliverance belongs to us!

People: We have been counted as unworthy. We have often been deprived. But, the Lover of Lovers calls us each by name. As a shepherd knows each individual sheep, so are we known.

Leader: This time and this space is sacred. The anointing oil flows freely to refresh, calm, and ease the weariness of our lives.

People: Robust and vigorous words of gratefulness pour forth from our lips. For all we have received and for where we have been brought, we bless the Lily of Every Valley.

Leader: Our God is truly awesome!

People: Stony has been the road, difficult have been the days, but Love has sustained us and the Chief of Every Tribe has been our help.

Leader: From generation to generation the name of the Shepherd has been held in high esteem, venerated by the ancestors, cherished by the elders, and precious to each one of us.

People: The Christ of Glory is king, to the everlasting praise of God!

Offertory Invitation

We have a glorious inheritance among the saints! What a treasure! What a joy divine! To this hope that we have been called. Let's remain faithful, both in our living and in our sharing of resources.

Offertory Praise

Spirit of wisdom and revelation, we come with grateful hearts. For your providence and care we give thanks. Receive now the works of our hands that your glory might be spread throughout the world. In the Name Above Every Name, we pray. Amen.

Benediction

Leader: Separating time is coming. The sheep will be sorted from the goats.

People: But God loves us all. How can there be any separation?

Leader: Feeding the hungry, welcoming strangers, providing drink for the thirsty, and caring for the sick and imprisoned are marks of sheep.

People: We leave to do the ministry of sheep in a world that is hurting and in need.

Leader: What you do for the least one, you do for the King of Eternity. Go! The God of Eternity, the Christ of Victory, and the enabling power of the Holy Spirit go before us. Amen.

8 · Special Days

LITANY FOR BLACK HISTORY MONTH[66]

Leader: In the beginning was the Black Church, and the Black Church was with the Black community.

People: The Black Church was in the beginning with black people and all things were made through the Black Church.

Leader: Without the Black Church was not anything made that was made.

People: In the Black Church was life, and the life was the light of the black people.

Leader: The Black Church still shines in the world, and the world has not overcome it.

People: Born in the agony of slavery and tyranny, the Black Church rose as the symbol of hope for every tomorrow.

Leader: There was hope for freedom in the Black Church.

People: There was hope for a better tomorrow in the Black Church.

Leader: There was the hope for deliverance from oppressors—NOW!—and not in the "sweet by and by!"

People: There was hope for a new day, a new beginning, a fresh start, and "a building, not made with human hands."

Leader: Our hope is yet alive!

People: Our faith is yet firm!

Leader: The God of the oppressed is our reality!

People: The invisible institution is visible and viable in and through us.

Leader: The Black Church continues to be the heartbeat of our communities.

People: And the High God of the ancestors remains at the heart of the Black Church. Thanks be unto God for our heritage, our history, and our hope.

ALL SAINTS SUNDAY
NOVEMBER 1 OR FIRST SUNDAY IN NOVEMBER

Revelations 7:9–17
Psalm 34:1–10, 22
1 John 3:1–3
Matthew 5:1–12

Call to Worship

Leader: The Holy Breath of Life whispers to us again.
People: We have heard the call of the Pillar and Ground of "Isness."
Leader: The Blood of Existence yet runs warm in our vein.
People: The Vitality of Being energizes our spirits.
Leader: From every tribe and people, from sea to shining sea, the people of God exist only because God is.
People: The Wondrous Fashioner and Sustainer of All is worthy to be praised. Amen.

Call to Confession

Pure, unblemished potential was poured into the first parents. Power, dominion, and authority was crafted into their very being. The wealth of the world was their legacy. The companionship of God was a daily delight. Confession restores us to the place from which we've fallen. Let's acknowledge our sin in prayer.

Confession

Holy One, we stand ashamed before your presence. You created our foreparents in divine design and gave them gifts to pattern after you. Their blood yet courses through us, but we have neglected and denied the storehouse of treasure within our control. When we stray from co-creating beauty and shalom with you, we have sinned. When we refuse to take the authority to change the situations around us, we have missed the mark of our destiny. Forgive us our sin. Blessing and glory and wisdom and thanksgiving and honor and power and might are due the God of the ancestors, forever and ever! Amen.

Words of Assurance

See what love the Creator has given us, that we should be called children of God, and that is what we are. Beloved, we are God's children now; what we will be has not yet been revealed. What we know is this: when divinity is revealed, we will be divine. When majesty is seen, we will be majestic. Our confession gives us this assurance. And this is good news. Amen.

Responsive Reading Psalm 34:1–10, 22

Leader: Our oral tradition has held sacred the deeds of the High God.
People: Before pen or paper, stylus or quill, the praise of the Majestic One was written within our hearts.
Leader: Praise, prayer, supplications, and songs have their roots in our genesis.
People: Authentic acclamation arises from the lips of those who have been delivered from bondage.
Leader: Words of encouragement have been whispered in the times of stress.
People: Yesterday's actions have been recounted with growing expectation.
Leader: The ancestors and the elders, our heroes and heroines, left us a legacy of faith and faithfulness.
People: The Deliverer's name is renowned in Zion. "Yes, Lord!"[67] has become our battle cry.
Leader: Oh, for a thousand tongues to exalt the ways in which the Strong Arm of Mercy has intervened on our behalf.
People: The kings and queens, the warriors and the gatherers, the griots and the history-makers of antiquity live on in us today.
Leader: Their greatness goes back to the beginning. Their offspring have inherited their connection to the Source of Life.
People: We did not just arrive on the scene of time. The Angel of the Journey has been leading us since the creation.
Leader: Savor the flavor of care and protection. Sense the aura of precious love.
People: Holy One, we will not let go your hand!
Leader: We bring the sacrifice of praise.[68]
People: We offer praise for our continuing existence with sheer delight.

Offertory Invitation

What can we give that would equal all that we have received? The amount is not measurable and God does not ask for repayment. We give because we want to return a just portion. This is all that is required.

Offertory Praise

Lamb of God who takes away the sin of the world, receive our tokens of sacrifice. Use them to help the world come into your glorious realm. Amen.

Benediction

Leader: The Lion of the Tribe has roared.
People: We have heard our salvation proclaimed.
Leader: The Beauty of the Tribe has been seen.
People: We have seen our legacy portrayed.
Leader: The Strength of the Ages has been uplifted.
People: The recalling of the exploits has encouraged our hearts.
Leader: Go to be the Great One's delight. The Antecedent enfold you, Today uphold you, and the Spirit of Life guide you in every tomorrow, with shalom. Amen and amen.

THE YAM CEREMONY · A CELEBRATION FOR THE BLACK CHURCH

Note: This worship service was designed and created by the author for Black Methodists for Church Renewal Sunday. It has been adapted here for use by any African American congregation.[69] Congregations need to announce early in February that this worship has a heavy emphasis on sweet potatoes. Members should be asked to bring sweet potato pies, cakes, muffins, and cookies, which can be blessed and then shared during the coffee hour. The worship committee should be encouraged to build an altar display featuring many different sizes and shapes of yams to be a focus for the day. Members will be asked to bring their contributions forth before the litany, in order that the congregation can see the many and varied items that yams provide.

Call to Worship

Leader: Today we gather to celebrate the gift we are as African Americans.
People: We celebrate our African roots. We celebrate our spirituality, brought with us to these shores. We celebrate our different ways of being that we share with the wider Church. We celebrate the High God who has traveled with us all of our days.
Leader: Today we gather to celebrate the gift we are as African Americans.
People: We affirm that we are on a journey, often from can't to can. We affirm that "stony the road we trod"[70] with stumbling blocks of racism often blocking our way. We affirm the God has been our help in ages past and is our hope for the years to come.
Leader: Today we gather to celebrate the gift we are as African Americans.
People: We have a song to sing. We have a story to tell. We have our heroes and heroines to recall. We have our own faith journey to share and our own rituals to rehearse. We have a God to praise, we have a Christ to uplift, and we have the Holy Spirit to magnify.
Unison: Today we gather to celebrate the gift we are as African Americans.

Hymn of Praise

"Lift Every Voice and Sing"[71]

Call to Confession

Now is the acceptable time. Today is the day of salvation. With open hearts and repentant spirits, let us turn, in confession, to the Ultimate One, who longs to be in covenant relationship with us. Let us pray.

Confession[72]

Loving God, we are an unfaithful people. You created us in your image and breathed into us the breath of life. We have marred your image and done deeds of death to ourselves and to others. Have mercy on us. Blot out our sin and forgive us. Purge us and we will be clean. Wash us and we will be as pure as new fallen snow. Grant us a new and a right spirit, we pray. Amen.

Words of Assurance

Jesus Christ is the source of our forgiveness. He died for our sin once and for all to put to death the bonds that hold us. We are reconciled to God through Christ and made equal partners in the covenant. God is merciful and compassionate, more ready to forgive than we are to ask. Rejoice and walk in the newness of life. Amen.

Joys and Concerns of the Community

Prayers of the People

Responsive Reading

Leader: The yam is a life-sustaining symbol of African American kinship and community. Everywhere in the world where we live, we grow, cook, and eat yams. It is a symbol of our diasporic connections. Yams provide nourishment for the body as food and are used medicinally to heal the body.[73] Today, as we gather to celebrate who we are as African Americans in the universal Church, may the symbol of the yam remind us of our strong roots, our hearty constitution, our necessity to the world, and our spiritual connection to sisters and brothers everywhere. The yam was the food of our ancestors; may we remember and honor their presence in us today. The yam is food for us. Let us give thanks for this plant of the ground, which draws us together. The yam is our symbol of hope for our future generations. May we always remember our heritage as African American Christians, with pride.

Leader: What symbol do you bring?

People: (The people bring their yams, baked sweet potatoes, yam breads, pies, cookies, soups, etc. forward to the altar for blessing.)

Leader: "What is wrong, old wife? What is happening to the [people] of the yam? Seem like they just don't know how to draw up the powers from the deep like before!"[74]

People: God of the yam, Creator of all things, we pause to give you thanks for the rich soil that produced our foreparents and was our homeland. The yam reminds us that you made us tough and durable, sweet and plentiful, resilient and tender. In your divine wisdom, you have nourished us and provided us with growth opportunities in all the places of the diaspora. Our roots have held secure. Our knowledge has increased. Our community has been saved in spite of dangers, seen and unseen. Like the yam, we have grown in the deepness of your love. We have sprung forth in the proper time and become a bumper crop, willing to share our joy of abundant life. We call upon your power today.

Leader: Too often we have forgotten and neglected the power we have received from you. Too often we have believed that we were ugly and misshapen, as the yam. Many times we have despaired at our colors, as varied as the yam. And we have been misused and neglected because of our durability, like the yam. Yet the yam has endured the rigors of time and the storm-tossed travel, from shore to shore. It reminds us of our story, and we call upon your power today.

People: We bless you for the yam and the many ways it has sustained us. As a protein staple it has fed us. As a tasty side dish, it has been offered with our leafy greens. And we have delighted in sweet potato pies and breads, which are our ethnic offerings to the world. You have blessed us, a misused and neglected people, to be living symbols of your sustaining grace and care.

Leader: We call upon your power today, Holy One, for the black Church and for its founders, who uplifted our uniqueness to the wider Church and made us more aware of our sweet, sweet spirit of celebration and joy, which needed to be spread. We call upon your power.

People: Majestic Sovereign, we call upon your power. For the black Church everywhere, its leadership and direction, as we continue to walk a lonesome valley and cry out for justice and long-denied liberty, we pray.

Leader: Lavishly Generous God, we call upon your power. For the people of the yam everywhere, we lift our hearts in prayer. As we gather to rehearse our faith story and to celebrate our witness to the wider world, we need your power in order that the black Church might continue to be articulated courage, visible dignity, strong endurance, and steadfast faithfulness in our service to you.

People: Name Above All Names, we offer thanksgiving for the ability to eat from the table, which is loaded with symbols of our heritage. We bless you for knowing us and calling us by name. We bless you for the power we have from you to be valiant, strong, gentle, and grace-filled as we face the days ahead. We bless you for the yam. We are thankful for food from home, which has been a constant in our unsteady existence. And because you have sustained the yam, we are assured that your grace will keep us and the black Church in the generations ahead.

Unison: We are proud African Americans, people of the yam. We will walk and talk with the power of God and give praise to the awesome High God always. Amen.

Hymn of Praise

"God Will Take Care of You"[75]

Scripture Lessons

The Living Word

Hymn of Response

"Remember Me"[76]

Offertory Invitation

People of the yam know what is right. We are required to love justice, to seek mercy, and to walk humbly with our God. People of the yam do what is right. We share from our resources in order that all the community might prosper. People of the yam give generously from hearts filled with thanks.

Offertory Praise

Yam Maker and Preserver, we are they who have acquired and mastered the art of stretch and make do! We appreciate your creative power at work in us today. Receive these, our offerings, and multiply them for greater use in the world.

Doxology

Benediction

Leader: You are African Americans, people of the yam, made of beautiful black, rich earth.

People: We are African Americans, people of the yam, brought by God to be witnesses and lights in the world.

Leader: You are African Americans, people of the yam, a gift to the Church and sacred to our God.

People: We are African Americans, people of the yam, and we will continue to offer who we are, for we are forever held in the loving arms of our God. Amen and amen.

Hymn of Benediction and Blessing

"We Shall Overcome"[77]

9 · **Appendix:** A Communion Service

COMMUNION LITURGY[78]

Call to Worship

Leader: Sisters and brothers, everything has been made ready. The table is spread!
People: We come to meet the living God, who is beyond our intellectual comprehension and is yet as close as our breath.
Leader: Everything has been made ready. The table is spread!
People: We gather to celebrate the risen Christ, who is God with us and, nevertheless, the One to come.
Leader: Everything has been made ready! The table is spread!
People: We assemble to be revived by the life-renewing Holy Spirit, who empowers our search for shalom in this unfriendly world.
Leader: In the bread and in the wine we will receive strength for the journey.
People: Everything has been made ready. The table is spread! Thanks be to the risen Christ. Amen.

Hymn of Celebration

"All Hail the Power"[79]

Call to Confession

When we gather to praise God, we remember that we are God's people who have preferred our wills to God's. Accepting God's power to become new persons in Christ, let us confess our sin before God and one another.

Confession

Eternal God, we confess that often we have failed to be an obedient Church. We have not done your will. We have broken your laws. We have rebelled against your love. We have not loved our neighbors. We have not heard the cry of the needy. Forgive us, we pray. Free us for joyful obedience through Jesus Christ, our Lord. Amen.

Words of Assurance

Leader: Hear the good news! "Christ died for us while we were yet sinners; that is God's own proof of universal love toward us." In the name of Jesus Christ you are forgiven.
People: In the name of Jesus Christ, we are forgiven! Glory to God. Amen.

Prayers for the Community[80]

(Response to each stanza: Sing "Kumba Yah.")
Leader: Someone's crying today, Lord. And the cries are of millions. Hear the crying men and women, boys and girls. Capture the tears of fear and suffering, the tears of weakness and pain, the tears of brokenness and disappointment. We are crying, Lord. Transform our lives.
People: Kumba yah, my Lord.
Leader: Too many are dying today, Lord. Too many die of hunger and homelessness. Too many die because of the systemic racist structures that deny the poor and enhance the rich. Too many are dying, Lord, because we neglect the power and gifts you have placed within us and told us to utilize. Too many are dying because we are not fully united in purpose and determined to stand together and be your witnesses. Too many are dying, Lord. Transform our lives.
People: Kumba yah, my Lord.
Leader: Someone's praying today, Lord, even while we wait. And we join with the faithful at prayer, even with our feeble and weak voices, in our broken and halting speech, in our wrestling and struggling, trying to believe that you hear and answer our prayers. But we are someone's today, Lord, while we wait in hope. We pray you will rekindle our spirits, touch us with your love, and empower us for the journey. We are praying, Lord. Transform our lives.
People: Kumba yah, my Lord.
Leader: For the healing of the nations, come by here, Lord. For the balm in Gilead that is needed for our wounded bodies and grieving spirits,

come by here. For the restoration of our families, the authentic coming together of our communities, and the salvation of our souls, come by here. For your Church, fractured and splintered. For your world, divided and in chaos. For the sake of the leaders you have placed over us and for the sake of Jesus Christ, oh Lord, come by here. Amen and amen.

Pastoral Prayer

Affirmation of Faith

We believe in the God of colors: A creating God who formed us from the dust of black earth. We believe that this God came in the form of a despised minority, named Jesus. He was born of a virgin, powerless, helpless, and dependent. He was rejected and carried our shame. Without cause they hung him high, stretched him wide, and mocked him as he died. He died, at the hands of a lynch mob, for our sake. Evil did not gain the victory. For Jesus rose, victorious over sin, death, and hell. We celebrate the risen Saviour who gave his life for justice and equality of all. We join his struggle as disciples. He has come and he will come again. He knows our troubles and journeys in us, day by day. We affirm our counselor, the Holy Spirit, who is the wisdom of God. Jesus Christ is our Rock and our salvation, the Ancient of Days and the Lion of the Tribe. We know he will come again! Amen.

The Hebrew Lesson

The Gospel Lesson

Hymn of Preparation

"Emmanuel, Emmanuel"[81]

The Challenge of the Word

Hymn of Response

"Majesty, Worship His Majesty"[82]

The Peace

The table is open to all who will receive the ministry of reconciliation and pass it on. Let's offer each other signs and symbols of God's shalom.

The Great Thanksgiving

Leader: The Lord is with you.

People: And also with you.

Leader: Lift up your hearts.

People: We lift them up to the Lord.

Leader: God of our ancestors, hope of the living ones, we offer you praise and thanksgiving because you loved us enough to empty yourself of awesome divinity and entered into our human struggle, taking upon yourself our despised color and position in life. You have walked our valley of sorrow and felt the whip tear the flesh from your back. You know what it means to be denied justice and to be abandoned by friends. So when our nationality is reviled, our color scorned, and our dignity defamed until we are without comfort or hope, we remember you.

You called together twelve and worked to achieve unity. You taught self-determination and role modeled hard work and responsibility. You healed and set free in order that others might maintain their economic development and have purpose in their daily lives. You are the essence of creativity and promised that greater works we would perform. It was your faith that allowed you to march with determination up Golgatha's hill. With help from one black brother, Simon, you carried a cruel cross. And on that old, rugged cross you became our sin and shame, sanctifying pain and giving birth to the universal Church. So, with all the company of saints, those who have walked with you to Calvary, that they might be raised to new life with you, we praise you, saying:

People: Holy, holy, holy, compassionate, identifying God. Heaven and earth are full of your glory; Hosanna in the highest. Blessed is the One who comes in the name of God; Hosanna in the highest.

Leader: Blessed is our Savior, Jesus. Bone of our bone and flesh of our flesh, who the cup of suffering did not shirk; who, on the night that he was betrayed, took bread, gave thanks, broke it, and said, "This is my body, broken for you. Eat it, in remembrance of me." In the same manner, after the supper, he took the cup, gave thanks, and said: "This cup is the new covenant in my blood. It is poured out for you and for many, for the forgiveness of sin. Whenever you drink it, remember me."

People: Christ has died. Christ has risen. Christ will come again.

As we eat this bread and drink this cup, we proclaim Christ's suffering and death until he comes. In the body that is broken and the cup that is poured out we restore to memory and hope all of the unnamed and forgotten victims of blatant sins. We hunger for the bread of that new age and thirst for the wine of the realm that is to come. Come, Holy Spirit, hover over and dwell within these earthly things, and make us one body with Christ, that we, who are baptized into his death, may walk in newness of life; that what is sown in dishonor may be raised in glory, and what is sown in weakness may be raised in power. Amen.

Leader: Sisters and brothers, Christ has made everything ready. Come and eat, the table is spread.

Breaking of the Bread

Lonely stalks of wheat stood useless in a field, until they were pulled together, bruised, crushed, beaten, and baked to become bread for a hungry world. When we break this loaf, it is our sharing in the body of Christ.

Taking of the Cup

Single grapes lay close to the ground, until they were picked, stomped, crushed, and smashed to provide drink for a thirsty world. When we give thanks over the cup, it is our sharing in the blood of Christ. This is an open altar. All who name Jesus as Sovereign, to the glory of God, are welcome at this table.

Doxology

Benediction

Leader: We have gathered for community worship and feasting. Now we are sent again into the world, with the authority and power of the Holy Spirit.

People: God has prepared a table for us, in the presence of our enemies.

Leader: We require nothing else for the journey. All our needs are supplied by an all-sufficient God.

People: A mighty fortress is our God, a shelter in time of storm.

Leader: The world has not changed. Evil continues. But, we are mandated by El Shaddai to make a difference.

People: We will cry loud and spare not! We will lift up our voices like trumpets in Zion! we will proclaim that this is the day of our God. Amen and amen.

Hymn of Benediction and Blessing

"My Tribute"[83]

NOTES ▨

1. Anita King, *Quotations in Black* (Connecticut: Greenwood Press, 1981), 38. John Brown Russwurm, "Editorial," *Freedom's Journal,* 16 March 1827.

2. Clevant Derricks, "Just a Little Talk with Jesus," © 1965 Stamps-Baxter Music.

3. Ibid.

4. Margaret Walker, *A Rumbling in the Land* (Boston: Houghton-Mifflin, 1999).

5. "Mary Had a Little Lamb," traditional.

6. John Thompson and Randy Scruggs, "Lord Prepare Me to Be a Sanctuary," © 1982 Full Armor Music/Whole Armor Music.

7. Matthew Fox, *Meditations with Meister Eckhart.* (Santa Fe, NM: Bear & Co, 1983) 88.

8. "Shine on Me," traditional.

9. Rich Mullins, "Our God Is an Awesome God," © 1988 BMG Songs, Inc.

10. Ken Barker and Tom Tenke, "What a Mighty God We Serve," © 1989 Word Music.

11. Leonard E. Smith, Jr., "Our God Reigns," © 1978 New Jerusalem Music.

12. John W. Work, Jr. "Go, Tell It on the Mountain," 1907.

13. "Kum Ba Yah (Come by Here)," African American spiritual.

14. Margaret Pleasant Douraux, "What Shall I Render?" 1975.

15. Smith, "Our God Reigns."

16. "Ain't Dat Good News?" traditional.

17. Isaac Watts, "Joy to the World," 1719.

18. "Take Me to the Water," African American spiritual.

19. Lyndell Leatherman, arr. "Spring up Oh Well, Unknown" (Kansas City, MO: Lillenas Publishing, 1982), 92.

20. Martin Luther King, Jr., "I Have a Dream," speech given in Washington, DC, 29 August 1964.

21. "We Shall Overcome," African American spiritual.

22. "There Is a Balm in Gilead," African American spiritual.

23. James Weldon Johnson, "Lift Every Voice and Sing," © 1921 Edward B. Marks Music Co.: renewed.

24. Bobby McFerrin, "Don't Worry, Be Happy!" © 1988. EMI America.

25. Thomas Moore, "Come Ye Disconsolate," 1816.

26. "Jesus is a Rock in a Weary Land," African American spiritual.

27. "There Is a Balm in Gilead," African American spiritual.

28. Charles Wesley/George Elderkin, "Jesus Is the Light of the World."

29. Thomas Dorsey, "Precious Lord," © Hill & Range Songs, 1938, renewed Unichappell Music, Inc.

30. Ibid.

31. Anita King, *Quotations in Black*, 8.

32. Ibid, 61.

33. Ibid, 70.

34. Ibid, 205.

35. W. A. Ogden, "Look and Live," 1957.

36. "A Motherless Chile," African American spiritual.

37. Mullins, "Our God Is an Awesome God."

38. Harry Emerson Fosdick, "God of Grace," 1930.

39. Charlie Barnett "Shake, Rattle and Roll," © 1940 Cherokee Music.

40. Alfred H. Ackley, "He Lives," © 1933 renewed 1961 The Rodehaver Co.

41. Joseph Scriven, "What a Friend We Have in Jesus," circa 1866.

42. Gloria Naylor, *The Women of Brewster Place* (New York: Viking Press, 1982); *The Men of Brewster Place* (New York: Hyperion, 1998).

43. Harold Smith, "Come On, Children, Let's Sing,"

44. Derricks, "Just a Little Talk with Jesus."

45. Zora Neale Hurston, *Their Eyes Were Watching God,* (Illinois: University of Illinois Press, 1978, 29).

46. Mullins, "Our God Is an Awesome God."

47. "We Shall Overcome," African American spiritual.

48. M. C. Hammer, "U Can't Touch This," © 1990 EMI America.

49. Brian Wren, "This Is a Day of New Beginnings," 1978; alt. © 1983, 1987 Hope Publishing Co.

50. Mullins, "Our God Is an Awesome God."

51. "Come Out de Wilderness," African American spiritual.

52. "Kum Ba Yah," African American spiritual.

53. "God Is a Good God," African American spiritual.

54. Dan Schutte, "Here I Am, Lord," © 1981, 1989 Daniel L. Schutte and NALR.

55. Isaac Watts, "Marching to Zion," 1707.

56. John F. Wade, "O Come All Ye Faithful (Adeste Fideles)," circa 1743; trans. by Frederick Oakeley, 1841, and others.

57. Thomas Moore, "Come Ye Disconsolate," 1816.

58. Schutte, "Here I Am, Lord."

59. George Frederick Handel, "Alleluia Chorus" from *The Messiah.*

60. Wren, "This Is a Day of New Beginnings."

61. Augustus M. Toplady, "Rock of Ages," 1776.

62. Mullins, "Our God Is an Awesome God."

63. Scriven, "What a Friend We Have in Jesus."

64. J. Fanny Crosby, "Blessed Assurance," 1873.

65. Scriven, "What a Friend We Have in Jesus."

66. Gardiner Roberts, *Quest for a Black Theology* (Cleveland: Pilgrim Press, 1971), xii.

67. Anonymous, "Yes! Lord" (anthem of the Church of God in Christ).

68. Kirk Dearman, "We Bring the Sacrifice of Praise," 1984.

69. Inspiration for this service was provided by Ms. Deborah Tinsley Taylor, a poet-singer-minister-sister-friend, from the Northern Illinois Conference/UMC.

70. Cain Hope Felder *Stony is the Road We Trod* (Minneapolis: Fortress Press, 1991).

71. James Weldon Johnson, "Lift Every Voice and Sing," © 1921 Edward B. Marks Music Co.: renewed.

72. Adapted from *United Methodist Book of Worship* (Nashville: United Methodist Publishing House, 1992).

73. Bell Hooks, *Sisters of the Yam: Black Women and Self-Recovery* (Boston South End Press, 1993), 13.

74. Ibid.

75. Civilla D. Martin, "God Will Take Care of You," 1904.

76. "Remember Me," traditional.

77. "We Shall Overcome," African American spiritual.

78. Adapted with generous interpretation from communion liturgies in *United Methodist Book of Worship* (Nashville: United Methodist Publishing House, 1992).

79. Edward Perronet, "All Hail the Power of Jesus' Name," 1779; alt. by John Rippon, 1787.

80. Adapted from "Asian Women Doing Theology," *Bread for Tomorrow/Prayers for Church Year* (Maryknoll, NY: Orbis Press, 1992), 60–61.

81. Bob McGee, "Emmanuel, Emmanuel," © 1976 C. A. Music (div. of Christian Artists Corp.).

82. Jack Hayford, "Majesty, Worship His Majesty," © 1981 Rocksmith Music c/o Trust Music Management.

83. Andraé Crouch, "My Tribute," © 1971 Communiqué Music, Inc.